My Year as Ozzy

Acknowledgements

Patricia and Robert Wrege, my brothers and extended family,
Hal Cook, Christopher H. Lee, Lin Caufield, Peter Boyles,
David Jones, Dr. Arnold Fox, Richard Whitley, David Jacks,
John Richards, Jackson Browne, Peter iNova, Greg Hollenback,
Robert Carl Cohen, Joe Manuella, Dr. Joseph Dilustro, Paul Bailey,
Ed Toutant, Povy Atchison, Daniel Lombardy, Bryan Lawrence,
Dean Rizzuto, Nancy Goodwin, Jeremy Borseth, Chris Power,
Hans Bjordahl, Jim Warner, Dr. Mark J. Barnes, Stephén Pacheco,
Harmon Leon, Barbara Hogenson, Cree and Donald Miller,
Ron Ruelle, Jay Petach, Rick Lewis and Michael Floorwax,
Elyse del Francia, Bea Fogelman and all of the
wonderfully warm and entertaining people
I met in the celebrity look-alike business

Oh, and Sharon and Ozzy Osbourne

*Dedicated in fond memory to
Peter (Austin Powers) Banks*

My Year as Ozzy

by

Don Wrege

MEDIAWHORE PRESS™
www.mediawhore.com

ISBN: 0615242804
EAN-13: 9780615242804

Queries regarding rights and permissions should be
sent to: donwrege@gmail.com
Published by Mediawhore Press™
www.myyearasozzy.com
Vi

Printed in the United States of America

Select photographs courtesy of Povy Atchison – povy.com
Special thanks to Marty Caivano
Print consultation: Wicked Sunny - sunnykapoor@yakshacomics.com

Table of Contents

Preface

"Were not this desire of fame very strong, the difficulty of obtaining it, and the danger of losing it when obtained, would be sufficient to deter a man from so vain a pursuit."
- Joseph Addison, English essayist, poet and statesman

Willie Nelson, Rodney Dangerfield, Neil Diamond, Jack Nicholson and Ozzy Osbourne walk into a bar. It sounds like the first line of a bad joke, but for me it was the start of the strangest year of my life. Just three weeks after I'd asked a friend to take some pictures of me as Ozzy just for fun, I was onstage at The Imperial Palace and hanging out with other fake celebrities in Las Vegas. Two weeks after that I was flown to New York by ABC, then to Chicago's NBC studios. It was, as Ozzy would say, a crazy train. All of this because people thought I look like him.

Even before the Osbournes had their hit series on MTV people would occasionally come up to me and ask if I was Ozzy. I didn't think much of it at the time. It happened mainly in crowds and especially at concerts. Once the television series hit I was harassed everywhere non-stop. I've looked like this for over twenty years while Ozzy's look has changed radically over those two decades. Now that he's totally burnt, he's settled on something that resembles what I wake up to every morning. Great. Ozzy Osbourne has hijacked my face, glasses and my hair...so I might as well make the best of it.

I was working for a Boulder, Colorado website company in 2002 when The Osbournes television show was breaking viewership records. One of my favorite clients was Churchill Downs / The Kentucky Derby. Each year we helped with the official Derby website and my job was to walk around "Millionaires' Row," the area where the rich and famous are seated. I would grab short video interviews with as many celebrities as I could with my camcorder, asking them which horse they were betting on in the Run for the Roses. It was a great assignment, especially for this transplanted Louisvillian. A chance to go back to my hometown on the most exciting day of the year there and wander around among the world renown with an All Area Access pass. It can get hectic, but I can't complain. It was at Derby 2002 that my Ozzy madness began.

Stalking celebrities, I managed to get interviews with Dennis Hopper, Alice Cooper, rapper P. Diddy, Bo Derek, Angelica Huston (who, once the camera was turned on, summoned an amazing sparkling presence), phenomenal actor Philip Seymour Hoffman, Backstreet Boys Howie Dorough and Kevin Richardson, country singers George Strait and Toby Keith, activist Robert Kennedy Jr. and actor Jerry O'Connell. My most embarrassing and humbling moment, especially as a film school graduate, was having to ask legendary director Francis Ford Coppola if he would be so kind as to repeat his well researched and carefully thought out response to my question, "Who are you betting on for the Derby race?" because I was so flustered by his presence that I had the camera in 'Pause' for his first take.

Even though I was wearing my hair in a ponytail and had a Kentucky Derby hat on, so many people called out, "Hey Ozzy!" as I ran around getting video vignettes that I decided when I got back to Colorado I would have a few pictures taken just for the hell of it. I made a deal with my photographer friend Povy to trade her a home-cooked eggplant parmesan meal for a photo shoot. She said okay. Now I needed my Ozzy outfit.

Boulder has a little costume shop downtown called The Ritz. One Saturday afternoon I dropped in and picked up a couple of costume jewelry rings, a few chains for around my neck, a gold cross and some black fingernail polish. (Ozzy's right little fingernail is a fine shade of onyx.) I didn't bother with eye makeup—I didn't want to go overboard just yet.

A huge John Lennon fan since pre-pubescence, I've been wearing round wire-rim "granny glasses" since the 70s. I took an old prescription backup pair to my optometrist Phil and asked him if there was a way to make the lenses blue. "Sure, fifteen minutes and fifteen bucks...I just dip 'em in hot Ritt dye!" Later, standing in front of the mirror, in a black long sleeve tee shirt, round blue wireframe glasses and a pair of black-with-white-stripes Adidas sweatpants, I took the rubber band out of my ponytail, shook my head and had to laugh. Damn! Hunch over, stutter and shake and I'm him. The more I laughed at my own reflection the more I looked like Ozzy which made me laugh even harder. It was almost a disturbing moment and it made me feel glad that I live alone.

The photo session went pretty quickly. Povy's a pro and helped me feel comfortable. I brought a folder of Ozzy reference photographs torn from magazines with me. We chose several facial expressions that I thought I could ape. Povy set the lights and camera, I'd glance at the photo, look at myself in a hand mirror at my side, pull my face to match the photo and hold the expression, then put down the hand mirror as Povy would take the shot. I still felt a little foolish about it all but we had a laugh and a nice meal after the shoot with her husband and brand new son.

When the transparencies came back from the lab there were three I felt were good enough to do something with. Since I build websites for a living and as a hobby the most natural thing was to put them on the Web. But now what? Email my friends? I did a Google search on "celebrity impersonators" that returned a ton of results. Who would have thought there were that many look-alike/imposter/tribute agents? I sent the first four on the list an email with the URL to my page of three pictures. No message—just the URL and a subject line of "Ozzy Osbourne." All hell broke loose.

I got a call the next day from Elyse Del Francia, an agent operating out of Palm Springs. "Honey you *have* to be in Las Vegas in two weeks at the *big* convention. Ozzy is *so* hot right now and *nobody* is doing him. We want *you* to open the show cutey-pie!"

Who would have thought that celebrity look-alikes would have a convention? What a blast though. I would get to dress up like somebody else, act outrageously with impunity, drink excessively because it's in character, pose for pictures with tourists, light up a room with a loud "ROCK AND ROLLLLLL!!!" scream and hang out with other fake famous-looking people in the casino lounge while the flashbulbs pop.

Sounded like a pretty damn good long weekend. I booked a flight.

1

Look-alike Convention – Las Vegas

"I thought it was a plastic toy so I just grabbed this thing,
bit the head off and thought, 'Fuck me...it was flapping."
- Ozzy Osbourne

I read the Web pages about the look-alike convention and it sounded like a lot of fun. "What the hell," I thought. I had some vacation time built up, I'd have a good time in Vegas, meet some people and find out if there was any money in this foolishness. At this point it was mainly about walking around casinos dressed up as Ozzy that interested me. Would it work? Could I actually fool people? What about up close?

"Do you want me to sing a song?" I asked Elyse, "No," she said, "but we'd like you to open the show." Cool! I was going on stage in Vegas! It was as exciting as it was absurd. Then it hit me. Uh oh...this was getting serious. I didn't even own an Ozzy record! All I knew of him is what I'd seen on his MTV series. I quickly bought a concert DVD and his greatest hits CD. I began taping episodes of *The Osbournes* (which was easy since MTV was running the smash hit in back-to-back blocks). I kept the episodes running in the background as I worked around the house so I could get in tune with his vocal delivery and accent. Sometimes when I was walking through the living room and saw him out of my peripheral vision, I had to admit to myself that the resemblance was astonishing.

One problem with my look was that my hair was way too long. Having not even trimmed it since 1989 when I left LA, it was twice as long as Ozzy's. Plus, Ozzy was dying the back of his hair deep red, so if I was going to do this right I was going to need my first haircut in

13 years. My office manager turned me onto a nice young stylist named Krisha, who treated me as gently as she could under the circumstances (I drank beer to calm down while the red dye set up). Once I was all done up nice and pretty with my brand new Ozzy flame under-highlights I decided to test it out on downtown Boulder.

I went from the salon to the rooftop of The Foundry, a local billiard hall and piss factory, to meet up with some friends. I was dressed in all black, my blue glasses and my striking new do, making sure that I was brushing the newly dyed red strands to the front where they could be admired as I sipped a beer on the roof garden. A drunk guy walked up to me, whispered "Right on man," and put a loaded one-hit hand-blown glass pot pipe in my hand. "You keep it," he said and walked away. "Now what the hell was that about?" I wondered, not realizing that it was the first sign the craziness had just begun.

In my research I learned that before Ozzy bit the head off the bat at a concert in Des Moines, Iowa (a legend he fears will appear on his tombstone) he bit the head off of a live dove in the Columbia Records offices at a meeting with the press to announce the release of *Diary of a Madman*. Most people think of Ozzy and the bat, but I had been unable to locate a suitable prop bat in time for the convention so I settled for a life-like and life-sized fake white dove I found in a hobby shop wedding aisle. Apparently people put these things on wedding cakes or decorate floral arrangements with them. I dubbed it my "Stunt Dove" as it would have to repeatedly suffer the indignity of having me jam its head into my mouth as I chomped down on the neck.

The final touch was Ozzy's black eye makeup. The Boulder women I know didn't really have a lot of great advice about eye makeup because they're all, well, *Boulder* women. The style here in town is kind of a laid-back, un-shaven hippie dippie natural. I went back to The Ritz costume shop for advice on how best to do the black "raccoon ring" around my eyes. This stuff doesn't come with instructions. The lady at the counter sold me on a little sponge paddle showing me how the black stuff was water-soluble. She demonstrated how to put the cake on first, then the powder. It seemed like a lot of trouble and I didn't have time to experiment with it but thought how hard could it be?

I used my Mac to create and printout some custom business cards, with a little picture of me dressed as Ozzy. I also made a "composite" half page handout consisting of two of Povy's shots with my name and the website URL beneath. Gathering all of my stuff I packed for Vegas.

Two and a half days at The Imperial Palace plus airfare was only around five hundred bucks. I wanted to find out what these look-alikes really think about while they're pretending to be someone else, ask them about the business side, but mainly try to get in the head of a celebrity impersonator. Does it mess with your psyche to be perceived as a different person? Thinking all of this might make an interesting article of some kind I called my friend Barb in New York who knows of such things, and asked for help writing up a Release that would allow me to use any interviews I did and any photos I took. I began to use the mission of creating a piece of prose for publication as the excuse to dress up and act crazy at 48 years old. "It's all about writing an article," I would tell anyone who questioned my sanity for attending the convention. I think the main motivator was that I wanted to have a good time in the process.

I arrived at the Las Vegas Imperial Palace around 3:30pm. Checking in I bumped into Elyse, the agent running the convention who smiled and said, "The press will be here in an hour to meet all of you so you'll want to get dressed." I freaked. I thought the press reception was later in the evening. I jogged through the twists and turns of The Imperial Palace (which seemed like three different buildings joined by a casino) to my room where I washed my hair and with shaking hands, put on thick black eye shadow—first the crème then the powder, all around my eyes. I painted the little fingernail of my right hand with black polish and wrote "O Z Z Y" on my left knuckles. Hanging several crosses on fake gold chains around my neck I was ready for my close up.

Emerging from my hotel room in full Ozzy regalia for the first time, I really didn't know what to expect. I chose to act the part the entire way (stumble forward, act confused) to see what kind of reaction I would get. At this point I was still torn about whether or not to carry a notepad with me and actually interview the other look-alikes or just roll with it. Luckily I was able to ease into the trip because the hallways were mainly deserted. I did manage to confuse a maid or two on my way down to the casino. I headed into the land of slots and cigarette smoke and shuffled through the casino to try out the Ozzy look. I got some turned heads, a few "Hey Ozzy's!" and a request for a picture. This seemed to be going well enough. Up ahead I noticed Willie Nelson talking to Neil Diamond at one of the bars at the edge of the action. Stumbling up in character I shook their hands and asked "Has the press reception started?" They were laid back, obviously pros at this compared to me. I ordered a round of drinks— I was a bit over-eager and it showed.

The reception was on the floor above us and riding the escalator on the way up I enjoyed making Ozzy expressions (arms out like Dracula, crazy open mouth smile) for the folks coming down the other side. I grabbed my convention badge from Paul McCartney at the table outside and ventured into the room where producer Dan Gore was making last minute stage arrangements with the people in that evening's showcase. "Hi, I'm Ozzy from Boulder, Colorado." He didn't even look up from his writing, "We're putting you on first. You just go out there and do your Ozzy thing and then get off." I handed him a CD I'd burned of the Pat Boone version of *Crazy Train* that was being used as the intro tune to *The Osbournes* teevee show. "Okay," I said, "I'll yell "Rock and roll and run around and deliver a line or two." He nodded and I headed for the food.

The press started to huddle around the hors d'ourves and the cash bar. I grabbed a Bud, something fried from a steam table and scoped out the room. There was a Britney Spears, a couple of Michael Jacksons, a lonely looking Charlie Chaplain ("Does anyone really care about Charlie Chaplain anymore?" I wondered), a dead-on Elizabeth Taylor, a Kenny Rogers or two, a Barbara Striesand, Kramer from Seinfeld and a Lucile Ball ("Does anyone really care about Lucile Ball anymore?" I wondered). I was relieved that I was the only Ozzy there (so far) and I actually started to feel just a bit special, since only half of the "professional" look-alikes I was meeting were dead ringers in my opinion.

If I could come up with a funny line, I would have a better chance of getting my name in the paper. Having been a fan of Sandra Bullock's characters over the years I mentally constructed a concise rejoinder for the press. If I couldn't meet and seduce the real thing, at this point, something that looks like the real thing will do. Which, if you think about it, is the essence of the look-alike experience. If you can't have the real thing, *this* will be good enough.

The gathered look-alikes goofed for the cameras and I cornered a couple of newspaper writers with my lines about wanting to meet a Sandra clone and have my way with her.

LAS VEGAS SUN
June 25, 2002
Double take: Celebrity mimics on display at Impersonators Convention
By Jerry Fink

Ozzy Osborne look-alike Don Wrege came to the second annual Celebrity Impersonators Convention at the Imperial Palace over the weekend to find a Sandra Bullock look-alike.

"It has always been a lifelong dream of mine to sleep with Sandra Bullock," said the 48-year-old resident of Boulder, Colo. "The way things are turning out, I'm not sure that's going to happen. At least through this avenue, I might be able to sleep with somebody that looks like Sandra Bullock, and that would be good enough."

There were no faux Sandra Bullocks among the 90 or so celebrity impersonators, but there were some dead ringers for Sophia Loren, Cher, Tina Turner, Dolly Parton and Barbra Streisand. Kenny Rogers, with half a dozen look-alikes, was well-represented at the convention that was created to bring together performers and agents, and to help impersonators hone their craft.

I mugged for the newspaper photographers with my Stunt Dove in my mouth and had a thoroughly good time. The press reception was followed by the Talent Showcase. Elyse and her tech guy had put together a show of about twenty short acts and I was to be the first out to open the show. The theater was "dark" that night (it was Sunday) so we had the place to ourselves. It was a friendly group of about 100 people that only filled the first few rows. Since I was to go on first I went directly backstage, nodding to a stagehand and checking out the ambiance. The stage was dressed for the resident "The Legends of Entertainment" show. We were told not to touch anything, just stand out in front of their stuff.

I paced back and forth backstage practicing the lines I'd just made up in my head. I wasn't nervous so much as ready to go. C'mon. Let me out there. After a while the show started with Elyse providing the opening introduction. She looked in my direction and I ran onto the stage yelling "Rock and roll!!! How are ya!" The best I could come up with was, after yelling and running back and forth, lapsing into "Confused Ozzy" saying in a befuddled voice, "I don't know what's happening…I think I'm going nutters…I thought I was seeing double! I saw two Madonnas, two Michael Jacksons and two fucking Kenny Rogers….then I realized…I was just backstage!" There was scattered applause and a few laughs. It wasn't very funny stuff, but it was all I could think of at the moment and under pressure. I felt I'd done his voice pretty well.

I came right off stage and back into my seat in the audience to watch the rest of the show. The Rodney Dangerfield was a riot, (sample: "So my old lady says after sex 'No more of that weird finger in the butt stuff—and I said what's it to you?—it's my finger and my butt!"), as was the George Bush (sample: "Clinton didn't help much with the Middle East…when he heard about the Gaza Strip he wanted a table dance"). The fake Britney performed with gusto and even pulled off a Velcro costume change mid-bit, abusing our privileges and throwing her outfit upon the Legends of Entertainment stage area. The quality level of the imposters really ran the gamut. One of the country singer look-alikes I didn't recognize couldn't sing, but I guess he looked like the star whoever that was. I was impressed with some and cringed at others, more than once wondering, "What are they THINKING?" But I had to temper it with the same question aimed at myself.

By the end of the talent showcase I had a decent beer buzz going and nothing to do with the rest of my evening. It was after midnight and I figured Las Vegas was just coming alive. I grabbed a cab and told the driver "Hard Rock Café," and we headed out—me in full Ozzy regalia and high from my first on-stage Las Vegas debut. When the cab driver stopped in front of the Hard Rock I thought he had the wrong door. All the lights were off. The main room was dark (duh…it was Sunday). By the time I'd surveyed the scene the cab had driven off. "Shit," I thought, and walked inside. There was a guy standing in the hallway and before I had a chance to ask him where the action was a couple of girls emerged from the restroom yelling "Ozzy! Hey Ozzy Osbourne!" These two were gorgeous, in their mid-twenties I surmised, full of energy that seemed a bit chemical, talking and acting quite loud and lively. A skinny blonde with a bare midriff and a beautiful brunette with more of a sophisticated manner, both seeming to be having an incredibly good time. The guy looked concerned.

"Nah, I'm not Ozzy," I told them, "I'm just a fake looking for someplace to make trouble. I didn't know the Hard Rock was closed." "Well the main room is," the brunette said, "But the bar is open. Hey, we'll take you somewhere that's happening, follow us." The guy looked a bit irritated but walked with us anyway through the Hard Rock bar. As we worked our way from the back to the front there were all sorts of shouts of recognition. "Ozzy!" The two girls were enjoying it. I just stared at the backs of their heads, afraid to destroy the illusion, and followed along waving occasionally at someone in the crowd shouting my new name.

We got to the parking lot and the brunette said, "Let's go to The House of Blues. That's where everybody is on Sunday nights." "I'm not getting in your car," the guy said, even more irritated. My first thought was "That's strange, he was *with* them!" I went with the flow, which is odd for me, since I'm a chickenshit, and asked no questions. Hey, what happens in Vegas stays in Vegas right? Climbing into the backseat of the brunette's new SUV, the bare midriff blonde jumped in the front and continued her accelerated non-stop monologue uninterrupted. I thought to myself that the only way I could blow this situation was by saying the wrong thing. I decided that speaking only when spoken to would be the safest way for me not to screw up. The brunette drove like a maniac. The blonde chattered like a rattlesnake. The evening was beginning to look encouraging.

As we careened at breakneck speed toward The House of Blues the blonde put Eminem's disc in the dashboard CD player and pumped up the volume. I noticed two changes of clothes hanging on the rear door hook, but hey…lots of people take a bunch of clothes around I guess. Whatever. The brunette turned around and shouted over the rap music "I'll bet you didn't think you would be kidnapped by a couple of women tonight did you?" I didn't need to respond because she had already joined the blonde in singing along with the CD. The girls seemed to be in a little world of their own and were enjoying themselves immensely. I just sat quietly in the back, trying not to say anything lame, digging on the fact that two beautiful women were driving me around. When it came to the speaking part of the song, "Daddy, what are you doing?" she shouted along with it, turning to the brunette saying, "How many times did you say THAT growing up?" At that point I got an uncomfortable sense that these girls were somehow "professionals" and had had a rough road getting there. At least the blonde. The super-model quality brunette had an air of indifference, yet she was obviously calling the shots, running the show, tasking the blonde and making the decisions. She had the wheel.

We arrived at The House of Blues but took several complete tours of the parking structure because the Eminem song was still playing, "It's my favorite," the brunette said, "I want to listen to it again." We finally parked and they again instructed me. "Stay about ten feet behind us and let us do the talking." Okay. Easy enough. Life is but a dream.

As we approached the front entrance of The House of Blues I noticed a long line of people waiting to get in on the left, and a VIP door on the right. The girls made a beeline for the VIP door. I looked at my feet and shuffled up at the prescribed distance behind them. I stood weaving, waving at the line of people in the "tourist" line across the way with a few waving back. The girls, negotiated with the doorman, motioning back at me from time to time. The doorman looked unconvinced. Suddenly the velvet rope was unhooked. The blonde turned and said, "Come on." Looking at the floor I mumbled to the doorman in Ozzyspeak, "Thankyouverymuchgodblessyou," as I passed through. He ignored me.

Inside, the club was thumping and bumping with the sound of a deejay on stage and lit by pulsating stabs of colorful spotlights. It was a sonic and sensory overload that really helped pull off the Ozzy illusion. The girls started walking me around the place, kind of parting the crowd as we went. There were lots of shouts of "Hey Ozzy!" and requests for photos. We kept moving. An announcer somewhere yelled into the PA system, "Ozzy's in the house!" to a roar. This was starting to get out of hand. We made it about three-quarters of the way around the club, passing briefly through the dance floor, when a large bouncer with a House of Blues tee shirt walked up. "Uh oh," I thought. "The party's over. I've been discovered." Instead he leaned in close to my left ear and yelled over the din, "Sir, management would appreciate it if you'd get up on stage and say hello to the crowd." I was shocked and amused, but keeping my head down I mumbled, "Sure, alright, rock and roll!" "Follow me," he said. We plowed through the crowd, his yellow "SECURITY" tee shirt being easy to follow.

Reaching the stage door the bouncer turned and stopped the two girls from coming in behind me, which I thought was pretty strange. There were other girls dancing on stage but the bouncer was insistent. "Just Ozzy," he said. I walked backstage leaving my lovely escorts behind. Going with he flow. The music was pounding at full-volume and the place was throbbing with dancing people. I walked up to the deejay on stage, stared at his gear, leaned over and said, "I'll just say a hello and split." He nodded, deep into his headsets cueing up his next transition. He didn't care if I was Ozzy or not.

The deejay thrust a wireless mic in my hands and brought the music down. I went into my yelling trip from a few hours earlier at The Imperial Palace, this time sans the bad jokes. "ROCK And ROLLLL!!! LEMME HEAR YA! GO FUCKING CRAZY!!!" The crowd screamed, I handed the mic back to the deejay and began to shuffle off stage, wanting to quit while the illusion was still working. The bouncer stopped me at the top of the stairway leading out. Again I figured I was busted. "Please have a seat," he said, pointing to a sofa just off stage and in the shadows. He invited me to watch the show from up there, and they were going to bring me drinks. I thought that it doesn't get much better than this, and what a weird day it had been.

That's when the two girls showed up and plopped down next to me. "They finally let us on stage…can you believe that shit?" At the start of the next song they both jumped up and started dancing along with the many other ladies at the front edge of the stage. I leaned back to watch, trying to strike a casual, yet brooding pose worth of The Prince of Darkness. The blonde pulled out a large cigar and lit it, handing it to me while she danced. I puffed on the cigar, pulled at my complimentary Budweiser and surveyed the scene. "What in god's name is the time?" I thought…mentally calculating how much sleep I could get before tomorrow morning's 9am make-up seminar. I didn't want to miss that seminar, I had to gain control of the art of face painting.

But the music and the dancing muses would make me forget tomorrow and I would get swept up in the action and would make occasional rings around the deejay and dance with the young people on the stage before returning to my chill couch. On one such orbit I handed the cigar I'd been puffing back to the midriff blonde, who without looking at it put the lit end into her mouth by mistake. "OW! Bad Ozzy!" she yelled. I was horrified—I'd blown it! She handed it back to me and continued dancing. Maybe I hadn't. I fell back on the chill couch and looked at my cell phone. It was after 2am. "I gotta get outta here," I thought. But I was having too good of a time relaxing and watching the madness. The brunette, dragging the giggling burnt-tongue blonde behind her, came up to me and said, "We're going to go get some ecstasy and blow and we'll be right back to get you."

Well that was it. Call me a chickenshit, but I was simply not into having a life-changing experience this evening with two strange and beautiful drug addicted women who were most likely professionals. Where had this Ozzy character led me? Things were happening too fast. It was too much to process. I'd left Boulder, Colorado that morning, and now I'm on stage at Las Vegas Hard Rock theater with the crowd convinced I'm a star, being invited to party hard with two drop-dead gorgeous chicks. No wonder Ozzy went crazy.

I made a decision. I didn't have the energy to continue on and be-sides (the logical side of my brain thought) I really wanted to attend that seminar to figure out how to do my eyeliner more than I wanted to pursue some X-rated dream sequence, so once they left the stage I did too.

What the hell, one last beer on the way out was in order. I felt I'd just made an adult decision, so I might as well temper it with juvenile excess! I walked up to the bar and was accosted from the rear by a raging drunk. "Hey Ozzy, I'm you're biggest fan man, have a shot. Have a shot with me!" He yelled in my ear. "No thank you," I mumbled in character, ordering a Bud Light. "Ozzy wouldn't drink Budweiser man," the drunk yelled in my ear. In my best Ozzy voice I replied, "You're fucking crazy!" The drunk recoiled and started over, suddenly even more convinced I was him. "Have a shot man...I'm your biggest fan." "No thanks," I replied, turning toward the bartender for help. "Ah c'mon...have a shot, just one shot with me." At this point I was tired and it wasn't fun anymore. I came out of character and said in a straight voice looking right at the drunk, I yelled "Look, dude, I'm a fake. I'm not Ozzy." The drunk fell silent for a couple of beats, looked a bit confused, then came right back at me with twice the insistence, "Oh c'mon man, you're Ozzy. Have a shot with me man! I'm your biggest fan."

That scene impressed me as weird. I couldn't talk this drunk out of me being someone I wasn't. I wrote it up to the hour, the alcohol and the town, (although this would happen again). When people really want to believe in something, they are hard to convince otherwise. "No wonder religion works," I thought as I hailed a cab back to The Imperial Palace.

I was barely intelligible through my tired drunkenness as I fell through a group of gaping tourists into the cab requesting the foreign driver to, "Just get me back to The Imperial Palace as fast as you can." With that we lurched out of the lot like a slingshot, running red lights and crossing medians for a terrifying ride through the night streets of Vegas. He was either insane or thought I was important enough to risk both our lives to save ten minutes. I gave him a twenty for a five dollar fare, and thanked the Lord I wasn't dead from a car accident or an unfortunate heart-stopping drug incident starring a blonde and a brunette. "I'm too old for this," I thought as I was headed toward the elevators.

Shortly after 3am I finally got back to my room and my black eye makeup wouldn't come off. I tried soaking it with a hot wash cloth using my Cetaphil face soap. Nothing was working. I was too tired for this, but didn't want to sleep in it. I kept scrubbing at my raccoon rings with the coarse hotel washcloth. I was starting to bleed "Eyelids are not supposed to bleed," I scolded myself. I was actually tearing bits of flesh off from under my eyes. "This sucks," I said out loud to the idiot in the mirror, looking even more forward to the makeup seminar where I hoped I'd learn how to deal with this situation. Or at least avoid gluing paint to my eyelids.

I woke up the next morning feeling like hell with a horrible gonna-hurl hangover, wondering if I had time to eat anything before the seminar. I went to the breakfast buffet at the Palace and tried to find a table far from any cigarette smokers. (Boulder has spoiled me, with its no smoking anywhere indoors policy.) I was reading a Las Vegas paper when I noticed a Robert De Niro look-alike talking to a Cher look-alike at a nearby table. He was laughing a lot. I tried to listen to the conversation but couldn't. I finished up my corned beef hash and scrambled eggs and went to the seminar room. I was in civilian clothes and was still feeling like an outsider. All these people seemed to know one another, but to my relief they were all exceedingly friendly and everyone opened up to me warmly. They were here to have a good time too.

At the make-up seminar, the Lucile Ball imposter was presiding in her civilian clothes. I didn't know she was "Lucy" at first, because the pretty blonde standing before us bore no resemblance at all to Lucille Ball. This professional look-alike truly does make an amazing physical transformation into the famous actress. In addition to being a celebrity impersonator she's a professional makeup artist and had lots of gear with her in what looked like fishing tackle boxes. Britney Spears came in and sat down next to me, which I found pleasant. So did Cyndi Lauper. "Ozzy's popular with the women," I thought, wishing I'd put some Altoids in my pocket—my hangover breath wasn't being helped by the cold coffee.

"No detail is unimportant," we learned. Put two or three details together and you have a convincing look that will put you over the edge," Lucy taught us. "Make your character's expression while you do your makeup. Have lots of reference photographs. If you can't fix a feature, draw attention away from it. Powder 'n' paint will make you what you ain't." She stressed the importance of having a good photograph taken of yourself in character by a professional portrait photographer.

Talking to the Britney Spears convinced me that revealing I was thinking about chronicling the look-alike experience for a magazine article would distance me from the participants. "My husband is an Elvis impersonator," she said, "sometimes we do parties together. I do magic at kid's birthday parties. Anything to keep working," (I thought, "Maybe get a real job?"). But she and her husband had the performing bug, and were working it together. They were certainly in the right town for this kind of stuff. "You wouldn't believe what rich people will pay to party their kids. They must have a lot of guilt or something," Britney said.

I had already learned something from the Ozzy experience: thank god I am not a woman having to deal with makeup. Makeup is a pain in the ass. No wonder chicks are always pissed off. They do it for the men I guess, then resent the men they do it for. But now I under-stand how women can go through rolls and rolls of toilet paper in the process, I used to think they ate the stuff they used so much. Nope. You have to use a ton of it to paint your face and then remove it af-terwards. It's insane, but kind of fun after a while to tell you the truth. It feels like you are transforming yourself.

The next convention event was The Legal Forum. As people re-turned from the short break (I found myself a beer) and took their seats, Elyse walked up to me and with a conspiratorial whisper thrust a folded piece of paper into my hand. "Be in room 835 at five o'clock for a photo shoot. Don't tell anyone else, this is a closed thing." She whisked away. "Well that's kind of neat," I thought and put the note in my pocket as the seminar began.

"What does no man want to have, but no man wants to lose? A lawsuit."

My grandfather, father, brother and niece are all lawyers. Growing up, I was cross-examined at the dinner table every evening. I was raised by wolves. As a result, I've always enjoyed writing my own con-tracts for my design business back in LA. I'm an ASCAP writer publisher so I know my way around copyrights. I've gone through the process of registering a couple of trademarks, and the business of en-tertainment law fascinates me. I was looking forward to this talk. A lot of discussion centered on whether "talent" (short here for: "look-alikes") should have agents or not. Obviously, the agents felt the en-tertainers should sign exclusive arrangements, but the consensus among the performers was just the opposite. It soon became clear

13

from the give and take between the panel of agents, a lawyer and one former performer, that agents were getting a dollar quote from the client ("I have two thousand bucks for a George Bush for the night of the 5th") and not letting the talent know how much the job was worth ("Are you willing to do the night of the 5th for five hundred dollars?"). The agent might get five grand and give the talent one, for example. The agents called this a "buy-sell," but the talent called it unfair. The lawyer called it possibly illegal.

The lawyer on the dais said that in California at least, agents shouldn't call themselves agents if this is the way they operate. "A true agent has a fiduciary responsibility to look out for their performer, and taking the lion's share of the money isn't looking out for them." I asked an agent woman in front of me, "Hey, I'm new at this, but why don't agents just take a standard percentage like twenty percent or something." She answered in an irritated tone, "If I had to take a flat percentage I might as well close my doors tomorrow," she huffed as she turned her back on me. I gave her a business card and a promo handout anyway.

There were a couple of horror stories to support the agents' claims that the talent needs them. One example was when Arnold Swartzenegger got stuck in India with the client not paying and no way to get home. Still, it seems with half the contract price and a round trip ticket up front, plus a decent enough legal document as a binding contract, a look-alike could tend pretty well by him or herself without an agent at all. Many do I found out. I learned that there are probably under two hundred people nationwide doing any kind of regular look-alike work. Only a few make enough to make it their full-time jobs (apart from the folks in actual regularly-running shows).

I was amazed that someone like the Rodney Dangerfield guy could actually copy the real Dangerfield's act word for word. "Isn't that copyright infringement?" I asked the lawyer. "No, the law allows for 'tributes' as long as they are not committed to a tangible medium such as physical recording." Wow…so as long as it's a live performance, referred to as a "tribute" and just goes out into thin air and an audience's ears, you can "be" someone else and do their entire act. Amazing.

John Stuart, originator of *The Legends of Entertainment* spoke after the Legal Forum and is a fascinating guy. He pointed out that if anyone gives you trouble about pretending to be a star, remind them that the stars are pretending to be someone else too. Somebody asked about an incident with a Michael Jackson impersonator in one of Stuart's shows. "When the controversy over Michael Jackson and the pedophilia cropped up in 1993, all of our Michael Jacksons were off the stages that instant. We even sent a helicopter to a cruise ship to get one. What happens to your star happens to you."

Stuart got the idea for a celebrity imposter show a little over 20 years ago and shopped it around Vegas to startled stares of disbelief. Why would anyone, in the city where all the biggest entertainers in show business regularly perform, want to see a show full of fakes? Stuart couldn't find a backer but so believed in his concept that he decided to roll the dice and "four-wall" the show himself, for the length of time that his own funds could support it. He rented the theatre and the crew, paid for his own advertising and talent and put "The Legends of Entertainment" on stage at The Imperial Palace— one of the only venues he could afford. He had enough funds for a six-week run. Twenty years later it is still running and still sells out. Stuart has expanded the concept to fourteen shows nationwide, including cruise ships, running six nights a week to full houses.

Stuart is a deeply religious man, (reflected perhaps in the clean nature of his Vegas shows, that contains no nudity or profanity). He had some words of wisdom that I took to heart. "As for the performers in my show, If you're not a good person, I don't care how good a performer you are because you won't make it long in this business. Let the character you impersonate be one of the many things you do; not the only thing you do."

The morning and afternoon sessions were now complete and most folks were preparing for dinner. I had to get to my room and get my Ozzy stuff on for the secret photo shoot, whatever that was. When I got to room 835 I walked into a session already in progress with Britney. We waved to each other like two "special" people, since we both were in the "secret" photo session. For the first time I was beginning to feel a part of things. There was expensive equipment everywhere. I recognized the photographer from the press session the day before. I found out later his name is Dewey Nicks and he's a famous rock and roll photographer. Somebody was sure spending some money from what I could gather. Dewey was cranking through expensive 120mm transparency film like it was tissue paper. He would set up a situation, shoot the shit out of it, handing one camera behind him blindly to have it replaced with a fresh one by an assistant. It was impressive to watch, and Dewey is a fun guy, who puts his subjects immediately at ease.

Elyse called me into the suite's large bathroom where professional make-up gear was strewn across every available surface. A lady sat me down in front of the mirror and started dabbing at my face with powder. I guess I hadn't done a very good job with myself, and I asked her for tips as she re-drew my darkened eyebrows. I felt pampered. Dewey snapped a few shots of the process. "Man," I thought, "He's burning film like there's no tomorrow." Who is this for again?" I asked Elyse. "They're from MTV," she said. Cool. I didn't want to ask too many questions because I didn't want to be lame, I didn't want to come off as un-professional and if this was a dream I didn't want to wake up.

Dewey directed me to go sit on the large, round Las Vegas tacky bed, (with the mirror on the ceiling of course) and Britney was told to "Go frolic with Ozzy." "Dear god, this is going to be fun," I thought as Britney, dressed in a *I Dream of Jeanie* outfit leapt onto the bed and started wrestling with me. Dewey clicked away madly. "Ozzy would fall off the bed," I offered. Dewey yelled, "Great!" and took shot after shot of me tussling with Britney, then falling onto the floor. "Wait, stay down there," he yelled. "Britney, ride him like a pony!" Within an instant she had mounted me. I started crawling around the room yelling, "Sharon!!" and Britney did a good job of staying on as we meandered around the carpet, flashes going off every few seconds. "Great, great! Keep going!" Dewey yelled, trading his camera for a fresh one. Britney was grinding her muff into the base of my spine, which was distracting me greatly from the task at hand. I don't know to this day if she was simply keeping her balance or enjoying herself and frankly I do not care.

The photos eventually ended up in the VHI-1 Video Music Awards program. The title of the program was "Church of Worship," and featured look-alikes from coast to coast in bizarre photographs. ("Worship" in this case being an observation about how VH-1 viewers, at least, consider celebrities.) The cover featured a fake Elvis coming out of a bathroom stall. In the laps of every attendee at the VH1 awards show itself, and who knows how many other copies circulated at the highest levels of the recording industry, me being ridden like a pony by a beautiful Britney while in the background, Elyse can be seen talking into the hotel phone, her light blonde hair luminescent in Dewey's backlight. I was so excited when I finally got a copy that I sent Dewey and his wife a thank you note. They were nice enough to send, all the way from Beverly Hills, a few 8x10s of me at The Imperial Palace Dewey had taken over the course of the convention. My favorite is a three-shot of me, George Bush and Snoop Dog that I keep framed in my office.

Elyse had come through again. She made sure I got a copy of the program and that my name was spelled correctly within it. This was real. I could hold it. There was even a quote from me inside about the terrifying incident with the gorgeous chicks at The Hard Rock! Somehow, and I know this sounds sick and foolish, but somehow seeing it in print made the Ozzy thing even more real. You have to understand that when you put on another person's "look" and walk around *as* that person, the effect becomes dreamlike after awhile. Especially in a place like Las Vegas, and especially with enough Bud Light. So what happens is already bizarre enough to be discounted by the rational mind. Seeing it reproduced in a publication somehow makes the dream a reality.

The second night of the convention featured an awards ceremony for the International Guild of Celebrity Impersonators and Tribute Artists (IGCITA). That there was such an organization was interesting enough. I sat with the other look-alikes eating our banquet dinners as the industry stalwarts rose to accept their glass star trophies. I was sitting next to George Bush and told him I was sure he'd receive some sort of recognition. "These things are all political," he said without the slightest touch of irony. He was right though. He was overlooked for a Clark Gable who wanders around the Universal Studios Tour lot for a living.

Later that evening we were treated as special guests for a performance of John Stuart's "Legends in Concert" with such fake performers as Elvis (of course), Celine Dion, Bruce Springsteen, Tina Turner, The Temptations, The Blues Brothers and others. It was a very polished and enjoyable show. We look-alikes had been seated in the front row and given drink tickets. I burned through my tickets pretty quickly and was happily accepting the leftovers from my new friends sitting nearby. After the show the look-alikes were ushered out first, and we emerged into the crowd waiting for the next show to great applause and many flashbulbs. We posed for numerous photos with happy tourists and I wanted to keep the feeling going, so as the crowd finally filed into the theater I suggested to Kenny Rogers, Neil Diamond and others that we go out on the town as a group.

So Marilyn Monroe, Austin Powers, Neil Diamond, Kenny Rogers, a guy who thought he looked like Hugh Grant but didn't ("Hugh" had to wear a name tag so people wouldn't ask who he was, which was really sort of sad) piled into shuttle bus and began our Casino Tour. First stop was the MGM Grand where we entered the lounge en masse as a band called Love Train was performing 80s funk. We caused quite a commotion and everyone smiled as the tourists lined up to get their pictures taken with us. Love Train launched into a version of *Crazy Train* yelling, "This one's for you Ozzy!"

We left after just a few minutes, not wanting to wear out our novelty and proceeded to New York, New York. We took over the piano bar as Neil Diamond was handed the microphone, doing a fantastic rendition of *Brother Love's Traveling Salvation Show*. I ran around clapping with the crowd. Then the piano man handed me the mic and started the chords to *Crazy Train*. I panicked. I didn't know the damned lyrics but I knew the melody. I sang incomprehensible lyrics to the tune (that might actually have been an authentic Ozzy rendition) and ran around like an idiot keeping the crowd pumped. We invaded and harassed a few more lounges ending up at a strip club outside of town around 2am. We were disappointed that they wouldn't let us up on the strippers' stages but the management was adamant. "We don't do anything to distract from the girls," was their answer.

Falling to sleep that night I reflected on what it's like to be "inside" the character and feel like you're "driving" someone else's persona around. It wasn't so much an out-of-body experience as just the opposite. Almost like a big crane operator must feel...you have control of this huge thing, but then again you really don't. It can get out of hand fast.

2

The Man and the Myth

"Sabbath is aggressive music for angry people."
- Ozzy Osbourne, actual rock star

Born John Michael Osbourne on December 3, 1948, "Ozzy" Osbourne's destiny was to include a trip from the depths of poverty in dreary Birmingham, England to the height of stardom. John Michael had a tough childhood. A new pair of shoes was a luxury. At times he worked in a slaughtering house gutting carcasses. For a while he tuned car horns and even did a stint in a mortuary. Things got bleaker in 1965 when his father died and Ozzy ended up in the Winston Green Prison in England at 17 for petty theft.

Ozzy's ticket out of Birmingham was a band he formed with his mates called Earth. Discovering another group had signed a recording contract with that name, legend has it that during a practice session someone in the group noticed that across the street a movie theater was showing a horror film. A discussion ensued about making "scary music." What started as a lark turned into a heavy metal legacy. In 1967, The Summer of Love hadn't reached all the way from sunny San Francisco, or even London for that matter, into Ozzy and the guys' lives. Their music was dark and dangerous. Black Sabbath became synonymous with a backlash against the flower-power day-glo hippie scene happening in the music industry at the time.

Black Sabbath worked Europe from 1968 until its debut album hit the states in 1970. Even bigger in the U.S. than at home, Sabbath was almost peerless in its command of incredibly loud, heavy, angry and comically demonic hard rock. They toured relentlessly and sold millions of albums. Never into the black magic trip themselves, the band saw it instead as an effective promotional angle. Ozzy told the press that the crosses he and the other band members wore around their necks were to ward off evil spirits their music was attracting.

Pose or no, Ozzy was bedeviled by his bad habits. As their fame grew, members of Black Sabbath grew increasingly irritated by Ozzy's drinking, drugging and unreliability. Deciding to kick him out of the group, Ozzy went into a deep depression and on a backsliding bender from which his future wife Sharon rescued him. Sharon bought Ozzy's contract from her father (who was managing Black Sabbath) for a reported 1.5 million dollars The situation caused a rift between the two as her father felt Ozzy was a complete loser—while Sharon saw him for what he could be: really, really famous.

Sharon's dad continued to manage Black Sabbath, now with Ronnie James Dio taking over as lead singer. Sharon and Ozzy formed the Blizzard of Oz band and released an album by the same name in 1980 that rapidly went gold. Ozzy became known not only for his crazed concert behavior but for his wild partying, over the top drinking and seemingly insane offstage antics. He claims to have taken acid every day for two years just to "see what it would feel like." "Blizzard" is a reference to "snow" (cocaine) as a tribute to the tremendous amounts he and his band were consuming during these times.

One drunken evening for example, touring in Texas, Sharon felt Ozzy had had enough and needed to go to bed. She hid his clothes in another room of the hotel while he took a shower, leaving him nothing to wear. Undaunted by this, Ozzy donned one of Sharon's evening dresses, a little bright green number, and went back out on the town only to find himself later in the morning pissing out the window of The Alamo, down the wall and on the heads of queued-up tourists. Banned from The Lone Star State ten years for this transgression, Texas finally let him come back in exchange for a $10,000 donation to the Daughters of the Republic of Texas and a charity concert.

"I'm not a musician—I'm a ham!"
- Ozzy Osbourne

In the twenty years he worked the road, and leading up to the OzzFests, (some of the most profitable rock tours going during the late '90s), *Diary of a Madman*, 1981 — *Speak of the Devil*, 1982, Sharon kept Ozzy producing product and selling concert tickets. The Osbournes had managed to amass a fortune through hard work and constant touring. They had a lot to show for it, including a very nice mansion in Beverly Hills.

It was an episode of MTV's *Cribs*, filmed at the Osbourne's house that gave Sharon an idea. The episode included Ozzy failing to use a normal television remote control and pleading with Kelly not to get a tattoo (Ozzy's covered in them). The family was so quirky, Ozzy so hilarious stumbling through his daily life, that it struck an augmented chord with the viewing audience both young and old. With the Osbourne family's enthusiastic and non-stop use of the colloquial term, "fuck," the show's soundtrack was peppered with "bleeps" as censors blocked its use—but everyone knew what was being said and after awhile the sheer repetition of the beeps became humorous. What was originally envisioned as a three-week mini-series became a smash hit lasting three entire seasons.

The Osbourne machine had thrived by acknowledging and promoting the anti-hero demonic devil that was the onstage Ozzy. Yet the real John Michael Osbourne is no more Dracula-like than Bela Legosi on his day off. Three decades of image-building Ozzy into the so called "Prince of Darkness" had planted in the public consciousness a picture that contrasted sharply with the lovable bumbling MTV father, confused within a sea of frenzied youthful activity, accompanied by the lilting laugh of Sharon, the matriarch who runs it all.

In March of 2002 the series had its debut and soon was the highest rated show in cable history up to that point.

Osbournes Up for More "Osbournes"

by Joal Ryan E! Online
Jul 8, 2003, 5:15 PM PT

The Osbournes' first season, running from March-May 2002, was a "media feeding frenzy," as the network put it. The wholly ordinary antics of Ozzy's 90210-based brood (See Ozzy pick up dog poop! Hear Kelly and Jack argue!) averaged about 8 million viewers--a monster number for a cable show.

To call the show's success a phenomenon would be to understate what this new Ozzymania generated for eight to twelve months. A solid 33-year career behind him, a 54 year-old rock star who wanted to leave the road behind and retire suddenly had a hit television series. His confusion was obvious and hilarious to behold as was his wife's obvious delight.

America adopted the dysfunctional Osbourne family in spite of their foul mouths. The fact that the kids could talk back to their parents and the parents would actually listen, was an odd lesson to learn from the Prince of Darkness. Articles were written about how well adjusted the Osbourne family actually was, (if you could move past their fondness for the 'f-word' peppering each sentence.) Things started happening fast—the Osbournes were in the paper every week. It reminded me of Beatlemania in the mid 60s. In April of '02 Ozzy was awarded a star on Hollywood Boulevard. Marilyn Manson gave him a kiss and his shy eldest daughter Aimee made a brief appearance.

In May, Ozzy was taken to the White House Correspondents Dinner by Fox Television's Greta Van Susteren. The President of the United States addressed Ozzy from the podium, "What a fantastic audience we have tonight," president Bush said. "Washington power brokers, celebrities, Hollywood stars, Ozzy Osbourne." [Laughter] "the thing about Ozzy is, he's made a lot of big hit recordings — *Party With the Animals, Sabbath Bloody Sabbath, Face in Hell, Black Skies,* and *Bloodbath in Paradise,* —Ozzy...mom loves your stuff."

In June Ozzy had the thrill of his life when he was asked to meet and entertain Queen Elizabeth II at Buckingham Palace. (He respectfully refrained from mooning the audience, one of his trademark concert moves.)

It was if a rocket had been tied to his back. Ozzy was everywhere. His, and his family's new MTV images, were manufactured in a multitude of media. Dolls, posters, underwear, tee shirts, lunchboxes, key chains, even air fresheners. Every sort of geegaw you can think of had "The Osbournes" distinct brand on it, all made in China. I wonder what the Chinese line workers thought who were painting tiny eyebrows, lips and crosses on hundreds of Ozzy dolls all day. "Who is this man who has so many statues of him...he must be a very important religious person...I wonder what the bats are for?"

Sharon Osbourne successfully negotiated the second and third season for untold millions of dollars. The family wouldn't have any privacy, but she would sure have a budget for shopping. Ozzy seemed to like the attention, and at times it looked like he was purposely acting befuddled as the cameras rolled. The self-professed rock and roll "ham" actually threw a baked ham through the sliding glass door of neighbor Pat Boone's house during one episode, when the Boone's had complained about the noise coming from the Osbourne estate.

You should never let go of your dreams. Mine came true and more. People ask if I could do it all again would I do it differently? Fuck off—I had a ball.
- Ozzy Osbourne

Me? My dream for as long as I can remember was to someday be famous. As the youngest of three boys in a family of five I learned how to fight for attention. Luckily I was born into a musical family, everyone played something, so once I got the attention sometimes I could keep it with a piano performance or a made-up song. Both of my older brothers were in bands growing up, and often on their band jobs I'd be the kid working the lights, feeling proud to boast "I'm with the band!" as I helped lift a Hammond B3 onto a truck.

For my 10th birthday on February 6th 1964, a friend of my father's, Mr. Hal Cook who was vice president at Capitol Records at the time, sent my two brothers and me something we'd never seen before: a full-on album promotional kit that happened to be for an album called *Meet the Beatles*. The promo package contained the record, 8x10 glossy photos, an official Beatles wig, biographical background on each Beatle (with George's bio listed as John's and vice-versa), a Beatle-branded 45rpm singles carrying sack and an edition of the industry newspaper *Radio & Records* entirely devoted to The Beatles.

Meet the Beatles was the clarion call of The British Invasion and the beginning of a show business phenomenon. I played the record incessantly and learned to sing along with all of the songs. Three days after receiving this mind-blowing promo-pack and becoming an instant Beatle fan...the Fab Four appeared for the first time on the Ed Sullivan show. My life changed dramatically because of that performance. I decided I needed to grow my hair long and learn to play guitar—along with millions of other American kids.

I craved attention so much that I would write letters to the editors of *Superman* comics, *16 Magazine*, Lloyd Thaxton's *Tiger Beat*, *Creem* and *Datebook* magazines just to see my name in print. At the age of 15 I was watching a locally produced "teen" program on the Louisville CBS-TV affiliate WHAS-TV one Saturday morning and found it so lame I composed a letter to the station's general manager attacking the show from "a teenager's perspective." My father got a phone call from the show's director and I thought I was in trouble. I ended up being invited to do the show each week as "The Hippie" panel person for the next two years. Through two summer seasons, each Saturday on *Here's Now!* with adult host Van Vance,. I was given the opportunity to shoot, edit and provide live voice-over narration for short 16mm mini-documentaries on the air. Now that I had landed on local television, I felt that nationwide fame was my destiny.

I asked the director if I could have some WHAS stationery to write all the record labels I could think of telling them that I was reviewing teen pop records on a weekly television show. He did, I did, and to my absolute delight, I began receiving regular shipments of promo albums and singles along with publicity packages. I was not only getting new free music, but was learning how it was being marketed too. It was an enlightening education. However, being on television every week at 16 years of age had expanded my head to the point where no one in my family wanted to hear me talk about it.

I spent my teen years dreaming of becoming a rock star. I had various basement and garage bands, played the high school talent shows and got beat up by the football team for having long hair. In my never ending quest for maximum attention, I got thrown out of my own group for insisting I be the only performer in all white, and the rest of the group would dress in all black. (To me this made perfect sense but the other guys didn't share my vision.)

By my high school graduation (1972) I'd been asked by my older brother to join the band he was in, which would have meant I wouldn't be able to start college. My parents stepped in with stern warnings about never supporting me in any way shape or form again if I chose that road, so I entered film school at Southern Illinois University to learn a skill I could "fall back on." Since I was already creating animated 8mm in my basement and live action 16mm documentaries for WHAS-TV, by the time I started my freshman year I soothed myself with the thought that knowing more about the mechanics of fame would help me assure my achievement of it. Plus Hollywood was not only the filmmaking Mecca but had become the center of the recording industry as well (as it moved west from New York). I felt everything would surely all come together for me in Los Angeles.

Film school was great, but I still wanted to be a rock star first and a filmmaker second. I discussed at length, with my songwriting partner Chris, ways to incorporate films into live performances (this was 1974). My plan upon graduation in 1976, was to have my wife, whom I had married when we were both juniors in college, get a job as a school teacher as close to Los Angeles as possible and I would write songs and become famous. I managed to talk her into this somehow but it didn't last very long—about six weeks—then I was told in no uncertain terms to get a job.

After working a couple of miserable Orange County jobs, writing songs in the evenings, I got a break. I landed a gig doing media projects in the heart of Los Angeles at a cool place with a silver business card called Metavision. The commute was ridiculous (about an hour each direction), but I didn't care. I would even take the long way so I could drive past the HOLLYWOOD sign.

Metavision, in 1979, was an earnest group of hippies dedicated to saving the world through the use of automated slide projectors and marijuana. Their offices were located across from Farmer's Market and around the corner from the CBS Television Studios. After producing a complex product presentations for Kenwood Electronics, I had shown myself to the "Meta-four" (the owners) to be responsible and well organized. These were traits needed at Metavision at the time (every day at 5pm we had a communal "smoke break" in the conference room and then would usually work late into the night, giggling at one another and listening to tunes of the day cranked up to ridiculously high volume levels).

Only a couple of months into the job Theo the president called me into the conference room. "Mr. Wrege, your timing is pretty good." Metavision had just landed the contract to produce the automated multi-projector slide work for *Always Elvis*, a traveling multimedia extravaganza marking the first anniversary of the King's death. (*Saturday Night Live* did a skit spoofing us called "Elvis' Coat" that consisted of a gold lame' coat on a mic stand being waved back and forth to Elvis' hits.) Metavision was to be working directly under Vernon Presley (Elvis' dad), manager Col. Parker and concert promoter Jerry Weintraub. "Now we're getting somewhere," I thought. My dream was to become a rock star of course, and now I was working with the manager of one of the world's biggest (albeit dead). Plus, I'd get to go to Graceland—the mountain top! (this was over a year before the general public was allowed through for carefully guided tours). I was going to hang out with Vern!

I'd never felt closer to someone else's fame than when I sat on the floor of Elvis' trophy room, with Memphis Mafia member Joe Esposito going through old black and white photographs. Joe started to cry. "Elvis loved his fans, man," he said, as I left the room to wander around, allowing Joe a little privacy. The loss was still fresh for him and obviously a tremendous one. I walked out into the hallway adjacent to the Trophy Room that was lined with glass cabinets with memorabilia on display and framed awards from foreign dignitaries on the wall.

The *Always Elvis* multi-media extravaganza was the result of Col. Parker having previously negotiated a contract with the Las Vegas Hilton for an Elvis performance as the opening event for the newly constructed Pavilion building, built for concerts and boxing matches. That was the plan, but the Big E didn't play along having inconveniently "left the building" for good. I'm guessing that the Colonel had received an advance to seal the deal. Since it was most likely a cash-for-a-handshake "contract" (which Parker was famous for) the Colonel had some leverage.

Parker, being a hard-driving businessman, was still going to honor the agreement godammit—even if it was with a canned tribute to Elvis instead of the real live person. Parker was going to demand the same amount of money for our multi-media show as he would have gotten for the concert. Even after Elvis' death it was clear from the reaction of the hotel staff that the Colonel still carried a lot of influence. When we got to the Las Vegas Hilton *Always Elvis* banners had been strung on every available light pole and hotel wall.

The *Always Elvis* premiere turned into a weeklong fan event with our two hour-long show running every two and a half hours. The show was comprised of 28 slide projectors, 5 synchronized 16mm projectors and a concert sound system. Many fans sat through the show more than once. With five screens of action it was almost impossible to see everything the first time and Peter iNova designed it that way on purpose. As the week wound down I happened to be at the hotel's front desk when the Colonel checked out. He laughed when they handed him a bill for his floor of rooms. "I never pay at this hotel...give this to Weintraub," and he stalked out. (Try that sometime yourself.)

One of the songs we illustrated with multi-media was *In the Ghetto*. We used beautifully stark photographs of southern urban poverty licensed from LA photographer William James Warren. Because we'd put so much effort into this production, Peter iNova wanted to do a one-screen video version for ourselves. It turned out so well I asked for permission to use it to market Metavision to the major record labels. Peter and Theo said sure, as long as it didn't interfere with my regular camerawork (their main focus was on the home electronics industry—they thought pursuing the record labels would be a waste of time).

By 1979 music video was just beginning to gain the attention of the industry. The form had been used rather extensively in England but was catching on slowly in the states. I felt music videos would be more fun to work on than Pioneer Electronics sales presentations and the like so I pushed on, especially since my unhidden agenda was to produce one of my own. I cold-called all of the major labels, which was nerve-wracking for me but exciting when I got a bite. I asked to be put through to the department that handled music videos and usually hit a dead end. However at Warner Brothers Records I was able to leave a message for a Jo Bergman (who had worked previously for The Beatles and The Rolling Stones). "Hi, I'm from Metavision. We have a videotape we did for Col. Parker from the *Always Elvis* show. I can show it to you but only in person, because the Col. will kill us if it gets duplicated."

That was enough to get me a meeting. Ms. Bergman was very nice to me and liked the tape. As a result of this introduction Metavision ended up selling Jo a sixty-thousand dollar multi-media new release marking presentation. I was finally working for Warner Brothers Records! (Kind of.) I felt on top of the world every time I was able to stroll through the Warner Brothers offices in Burbank with even the slightest sense of belonging. I even had the opportunity to present and pitch the storyboards I'd drawn to label vice president Stan Cornyn and his staff in an executive conference room that was graced in one corner by a life-sized stand-up of Bootsy Collins in all of his psychedelic grandeur. They liked the concepts and we sold them the show. I was all of 25.

This new turn of events was what I needed to convince my song-writing partner Chris to move out to LA any way he could so we could take advantage of my newfound access to the big time. Since I was in and out of the Warner Brothers Records offices often, and was making contacts and friends on the inside, all of the usual barriers to submitting material could be breached as I could physically hand a decision maker our product instead of having it rejected at the front desk. This, I felt, was huge. Meanwhile I used the same approach with Capitol Records and soon Metavision was working with their marketing and promotion people as well. I felt a momentum building up.

Chris used the same method I did a couple of years earlier and enlisted his girlfriend to find a job in LA so he could move there with her and write songs "for a living." Chris weighed 300+ pounds and I weighed 145. Since Laurel and Hardy had already been used, Chris named our two-man group: "OddS." We discussed various album titles *At OddS*, *Against All OddS*, *Good OddS*, in earnest conversations. I started stressing about exactly what I would say when we were interviewed on *The Tonight Show*. We argued how to split up the massive riches our music would make us. We hadn't recorded any songs, but we argued endlessly about what our first album cover should look like.

In 1980 I asked Metavision if I could take two weeks off to make a music video of my own. I invited Theo to produce the soundtrack. This was a tactical decision (involve the boss) but was an especially difficult thing for me to ask because I wanted total control. But my hearing has always been bad, Theo was a good audio producer and I needed his complete buy-in so I decided it would be a good move.

It was. Theo did a great job of pulling something out of the tune Chris and I had put together (*Dangerous Man*) that was actually listenable. Chris and I set about building a film around it. We fought over storyboards and beers and ended up with a budget of eight grand (out of my pocket), a shooting script, and a rag-tag team of out of work independents and former film school friends. Since the concept of the group was that Chris and I are opposites, he was to appear angry and threatening in his close-ups and I would appear happy-go-lucky, harmless and happy. For my ridiculous happy scenes I smeared Vaseline on my teeth (a trick I learned from watching a movie about

28

beauty pageants) so that during multiple takes I could still crack a smile without my lips hanging up on dry enamel. My production manager found a female actress for the bar scene who would only cost me $50 for the four-hour shoot. Her name was Cassandra Peterson and she was a comedienne with the Groundlings, an LA improv troupe. (I didn't know at the time that Cassandra posed as the stripper on Tom Waits' *Small Change* album cover, nor could I have predicted that she would go on to become famous as Elvira, Mistress of the Dark.)

Eight thousand dollars bought me two songs' worth of film in the can (for a two-sided single). My wife was not amused. I built upon my experience with the Warner Brothers project to hire a good video editor in order to get a quality final product (minus one day's shooting because my cheap cinematographer blew a roll of film). Convinced I was on the verge of success, I quit Metavision to go freelance, feeling they were standing in the way of my dreams. Mainly I quit so I'd have more time to devote to music. Now approaching 27, I was as old as a career in rock and roll would tolerate and had to get this fame thing moving a lot faster.

My preference was instead of getting a band together, lugging equipment around, having all the hassles of live performance while "building a buzz," OddS would be a "media band." It would be much easier—we wouldn't have to lift things, put up with other band members and their schedules, and our "appearances" would be electronic. The "videomusic" business, as it was known at the time, was picking up. We could catch a wave! Our music videos had their debut at the first Billboard Magazine Video Music Conference. Things were looking good.

Then we broke up.

But the angels sang one morning a year later in August of '81 when the *Los Angeles Times* ran an article about a new 24-hour music channel called MTV. That very day I FedEx'd the OddS video and promo pack to New York, not bothering to mention that the band no longer existed. Within a couple of months it was on MTV in normal rotation. I was shaking my ass on cable and over 1.8 million viewers could see it. That's a large audience and I petitioned ASCAP for a "special venue" royalty. ASCAP paid me two royalty payments of one hundred dollars each. For my eight thousand dollar investment I got two hundred bucks. I felt like I'd become a professional. The economics of the "success" weren't looking all that good, but the way I figured, the advertising I was getting was something I could capitalize on and worth well over eight grand.

The MTV video turned out to be the pinnacle of my show business career, not that I knew it at the time. By 1984 I'd divorced my unfaithful wife of 11 years, moved out of the Sherman Oaks house into a hideously expensive bachelor pad in Santa Monica, and arranged for studio space for my multimedia optical printer nearby on 26th St. at Colorado Ave. The freelance design and camerawork was doing surprisingly well and I was getting ten and twenty thousand dollar open purchase orders from Mattel Toys, among other Fortune 500 clients, on a regular basis. I'd formed a "divorce band" comprised of two film school buddies and the audio-visual guy from Redken Labs (one of my clients). Everyone in the group was an multimedia specialist in addition to being a musician.

In 1985 I ended up on the team that produced the fifteen-screen, thirty-projector show for Jackson Browne's 1986 tour. Not a fan of Browne's music at the time, and having a "tough year" after my divorce (read: drunk) I wandered into the first meeting with him loaded. We were looking through transparencies and discussing possible animation sequences. Everyone was hushed and in awe of the quiet rock star in our midst but me. "Hey Jackson," I sprayed at one point, "Why don't you write another goddam sensitive love song, put your pretty puss on the album cover instead of a weird picture of the Statue of Liberty and get back in the Top Ten?" Everyone gasped and went silent. Jackson looked up slowly from the light table at me over the rims of his reading glasses—then started to laugh. I learned over time that Jackson not only didn't need another hit record in his life (he was doing just fine thank you) but appreciated the offhand honest comment more than the fawning praise he was more used to getting. Somewhat ironic is that while I finally ended up working on an actual rock and roll show, at that point in his career Jackson's wild partying days were over. By the time I met him he was anti-drugs, a vegetarian, worked out with trainers, drank bottled water and I didn't see him take an alcoholic drink. In fact I felt the need to behave myself in his presence—some rock and roll party this was!

Here was a bona-fide celebrity, a folk/rock legend—a true LA star who preferred to be treated like an everyday nobody. It was opposite from everything I had imagined a star's behavior to be and it wouldn't strike me as significant until years later. At the time I just thought he was pleasantly boring and a bit too serious. But the more I listened to his music, the more I began to like it, especially the political stuff. Beyond the '86 tour I did a couple of other projects with Jackson over the years and consulted on his early Web presence. Occasionally I ended up backstage during a concert or two, which put me tantalizingly close, being in the wings *almost* experiencing real rock stardom. Standing fifty feet from the spotlight was very frustrating. I wanted to be in it.

I was inspired to put media behind my own band's music by watching Jackson's show and witnessing the audience's enthusiastic reception to it. This gave my life a new focus for the next two years. It also drained my bank account in the process. "Eyesongs," our little group, appeared in showcases around LA, playing Madam Wong's, The Central (now Johnny Depp's Viper Lounge), Club 88 and At My Place in Santa Monica. We lugged a six-projector multimedia setup with us and projected animated sequences on a large scrim screen while we played. Jackson was even nice enough to drop by one of the Santa Monica shows. It was a great presentation if I do say so myself, but a money-losing proposition. Even charging eight bucks at the door, which was a lot at the time, I was personally losing about two hundred and fifty each time we performed, and wasn't able to pay the other band members a dime. This was becoming old faster than me.

By 1989 I'd been in the Los Angeles area for 13 years and was tired of it. What was fun in my twenties was now a pain in the ass in my late thirties. Losing a wife and a house, having a car stolen, building then selling a business, almost being killed in an automobile crash that wasn't my fault—I wanted out. Leaving Los Angeles in December of 1989 was very difficult though, because it meant I was voluntarily hanging up my dreams of fame. I was quitting. LA won and I lost. I gave it a shot and that was that. I drove east out of town, tried not to look back and tried not to feel like a failure as I contemplated a life of obscurity that lay ahead.

I stayed connected to the music business in a tangential way by working with MusicNet in San Francisco in 1992, but this just caused me to be more depressed about the state of the industry. At work each day we heard everything the six major distribution companies released, and while I counted myself a huge fan of music, could only bring myself to buy about five of the thousands of titles I previewed over the course of a year. After 54 weeks in lovely San Francisco I realized that the situation was going nowhere and at the urging of friend Don LaSala, sent a résumé in response to an ad in the *San Francisco Chronicle* seeking a multimedia producer for the ground breaking Interactive Video Enterprises in Boulder, Colorado. To my surprise and delight I landed it. I was forty years old. Any dreams of becoming a rock star at this point were delusional. From here on out I would play for my own enjoyment or at best, try to sell a song or two to someone else. I was happy just to be on a corporate health plan. So much for fame.

Eight years later, Ozzy's show hit MTV. It just so happened that Ozzy, at 54 years of age, had settled into a look (long hair worn straight down, round "granny" glasses) that resembled me quite a bit—at least people kept telling me so. By taking advantage of the skyrocketing fame of Ozzy Osbourne in 2002, I was able to catch hold of a comet trail of attention, fun and fame that didn't belong to me but felt good nonetheless and took me places I couldn't have gone otherwise. Never setting my sites on imitating anyone or anything to achieve some level of public recognition, how could I not let this madness run its course and, in a strange way, experience something that was at least an approximation of what I had yearned for my entire life?

In the process I found out that sometimes almost real is real enough.

3

Live with Regis and Kelly

"My only ambition in the world is to go to Egypt, stand on top of the central pyramid and piss all over it."
– Ozzy Osbourne

Two days before I left for the Vegas convention, my friend Ed emailed me with a tip about the television show, *Regis and Kelly Live*'s annual "look-alike contest." This was to be a weeklong series of shows featuring ordinary people who look like famous people. The "rules" included a 'no professionals' clause that concerned me a little. Since I hadn't been paid by anyone yet, in my opinion that meant I wasn't a professional. I certainly had no intention of quitting my day job. On the Web page I'd put up for fun I clearly stated that I didn't see myself biting the heads off bats at children's birthday parties, (but I'd be interested in being Ozzy's stunt double on his tour). I was a rank amateur even if I was attending a professional convention. That was to be my position if challenged.

The *Live with Regis and Kelly* website had an email address for electronic submissions and I tried several times to send a picture and my Ozzy site's URL. They all bounced. I started to really freak because the deadline for entries was the very next day. Friday June 21st I overnighted a package containing printouts of two of the Povy portraits from my Ozzy home page. The deadline was that day, but I hoped the producers would be retrieving any snail mailed items on the following Monday.

While I was in Vegas I made no mention of the Regis and Kelly opportunity to the look-alikes I met there. Not so much because the deadline had passed—I just didn't want any competition or noise caused by one of them calling the show trying to get on at the last minute. I felt bad about this for a while but got over it. Was I actually starting to treat this Ozzy nonsense as some kind of professional thing? Protecting my turf all of a sudden? Did I even *have* turf?

The day after I got back from Vegas my desk phone rang at work. "They want me in New York for Regis," I announced to my office mates. I was stunned and my adrenaline was racing. Thinking "Oh my god, what have I done?" I immediately called my parents with the news. I didn't have a lot of time to worry about it since it was June 25th and I was to fly to New York on the 2nd one week later. I don't know why it took me a couple of days to figure out that I should publicize this news. By Thursday afternoon I had finally composed an email and spammed the Boulder *Daily Camera, The Denver Post* and *The Rocky Mountain News* with my fake PR release. Friday morning the *Daily Camera* reporter Andy Stonehouse, called first to confirm that I was indeed doing the Regis show, then asking me some of the standard questions (how long have you been doing this, is this your job, what weird things have happened, etc.). He also asked whether or not I'd contacted any other papers. I feared that because I had, he would drop the story so I said, "Since you called first you can have an exclusive…" He said, "Nah, if you have that just means we'd better move on this. We'll need a photo of you. How about over the weekend sometime?" "Sounds great," I said. "Just tell me when." "The photographer will call you,"

Bill Husted of *The Denver Post* called me later that morning with, "Well, this item has gone around the newsroom twice and ended up with me." He didn't sound all that excited about it, but after asking the standard questions he giggled at my quip about not being able to find any women in Boulder who could answer questions about makeup. I felt I'd given him something he could use.

Up to this point I had simply worn my father's dark blue London Fog overcoat as my "formal Ozzy" outfit. But for national television I wanted to do it right. Saturday morning I took my cell phone with me so I wouldn't miss the call from the *Daily Camera* photographer as I traveled south to Westminster, between Boulder and Denver, in search of something my friend Nancy described as a "reverend's coat." Ozzy wears them, sometimes using the wide pointy lapels to hang military ribbons. Nancy told me I could probably get one at the shop called Hot Topic in the Westminster mall and she was right.

I picked out a reverend's coat that fit—almost four and a half feet long, cut thin at the waist, swooping out at the ankles with exaggerated and padded wide shoulders. Pitch black, of course, with four silver buttons down the front that secure with loops. I noticed the store had a selection of temporary hair spray in a wide array of colors. "Mainly for raves," said the girl behind the counter with the jet-black glued-to-points hair and metal hoops coming out of her lip, ear and eyebrows. I chose bright red, to highlight the hair in back and underneath like Ozzy's. Goth Girl was very helpful in providing spraying tips. Add a couple of black tee shirts, two silver skull rings and I left about $150.00 lighter but, I felt, a lot Ozzy-er. "Might as well take one of these," the punctured goth girl said, handing me a VIP customer card with 10 of the 12 little skull icons punched out. "You're most of the way to a 10% discount." She might look like a character from a Tim Burton movie on the eve of a suicide but she was an excellent saleswoman.

Dragging the bags through the mall back to my trusty 1989 Mazda MPV I fondly call, "Bluebell the Love Van," I passed the Wilson's leather shop's storefront festooned with "50% OFF!" banners. "Ozzy wears a nice black leather coat," I thought, and not since I received some questionable fashion advice from a lesbian friend right after my divorce twenty years earlier have I owned black leather pants. About $200 later I had, thanks to the summer special, saved about as much as I spent as they say. But between the original costume jewelry, the makeup, and now this shopping spree, I was investing a *lot* in this lark. I went home and laid it all out. I checked my message machine for any word from the *Daily Camera* photographer finding none. Sunday dragged on, me spending the day packing and watching tapes of *The Osbournes*, and I never did hear from that photographer. "Damn, they've decided not to do it," I thought.

Monday morning I called the *Daily Camera* reporter about the photographer not contacting me. He apologized saying it was a big screw-up and could I possibly do it that evening. "Sure," I said, "how about the graveyard on 9th at sundown?" He laughed. "Sounds good. I'll have the photographer meet you there at seven." Delighted, I replied,

"The sun should be coming down behind the tombstones by then. That should be cool."

Monday evening I hurried home from work, did my hair, and put on the Ozzy stuff. I drove up toward the base of Boulder's Flatirons and was stumbling around 9th street looking for a way into the old pioneer's graveyard when I spotted the photographer. A lovely olive-skinned young woman named Marty who was packing a ten thousand dollar digital Nikon. I admired both. She got right down to business, putting me through a set of poses, working hard to get the flash fill just right. Even though it was going on dusk it was still hot, and I was sweating heavily underneath the reverend's coat. I was afraid the black makeup around my eyes was going to run. We timed the sun-down perfectly and I felt we had a good shot or two. The next morning I was to fly to New York. Marty didn't know if or when the story was going to run. I gave her my business card and she promised to email me if she heard anything.

I went straight home and packed methodically. Every time I travel I seem to leave something behind, and I was intent on breaking that habit. I didn't want to have to be running around New York to find a piece of fake jewelry at the last minute or anything. With a choice of my leather outfit and the reverend's coat, I couldn't jam everything into a carry-on so I was lugging my large American Tourister. I set the alarm for 4am figuring a half hour to get out of the house, an hour to get to the parking lot and a half hour from the parking lot to DIA. That would put me there at 6am for a 7:40am flight. I was thinking of everything that could go wrong (Bluebell has a flat, etc.) and hoping that I wouldn't let the Regis show down in any way. The producer's assistant had emailed me my itinerary:

```
United #418
8:10am depart
Arrive Newark 1:49pm

Bermuda Car Co.
212-249-8400 will pick up

Rihga Royal Hotel
151 W. 54th St.   212-307-5000
(call to confirm a non-smoking
room)
```

Leaving the driveway in the pre-dawn dark of July 2nd, more by force of habit than anything else, I stopped by the newsstand to pick up a copy of the *Daily Camera*. I put two quarters into the machine, took out a copy and flipped it open to the Local News section. Nothing on me. "Well damn...maybe tomorrow," I thought as I tossed the paper on the floorboard. It landed face down exposing the lower half of the front page that was commanded by a huge color photo of me in the graveyard, reaching creepily with both hands toward the reader. My heart stopped. "Is He Our Own Ozzy Osbourne?" the headline asked. A shot of adrenaline way more powerful than my morning coffee surged through me. I smiled all the way to the airport. "Unbelievable," I thought, "now THAT defines a slow news day.

Is he our own Ozzy Osbourne?

'Regis and Kelly Live' to feature Boulder resident in look-alike segment

By Andy Stonehouse, Camera Staff Writer
July 2, 2002

Boulder resident Don Wrege has been haunted by the spirit of heavy metal star Ozzy Osbourne for the past two years and now it's paying off.

Wrege, 48, said people had commented on his resemblance to Osbourne, the former Black Sabbath leader, but that the comments increased by a lot when MTV's "The Osbournes"—a reality show about the rocker and his family debuted in March. ..."The only reason I went out there was that I hoped I'd be able to sleep with a Sandra Bullock look-alike, but Cyndi Lauper was about the closest chance I got," Wrege said. "The whole convention was a goof. Going to Las Vegas is weird enough, but imagine doing it dressed as Ozzy Osbourne—I managed to walk my way into the VIP door at the House of Blues and even got invited on stage."

Cool. He put in my gag line about Sandra Bullock. I bought a copy of *The Denver Post* at the airport and found my picture on page 2. Another shot of adrenaline. Bill Hustead had written a nice blurb. The headline read: "Ozzy twin up to bat in NYC." I was delighted that they'd used my Sad Ozzy photo that Povy shot.

```
Boulder Internet guy Don Wrege looks like
Ozzy Osbourne. Isn't he lucky? If you don't
believe me, check out
www.ozzylookalike.com. If you still don't
believe me, watch "Live with Regis & Kelly"
at 9am Wednesday on Channel 2. Wrege is
flying to NYC today and will be on the show
in all his Osbourne glory.

Wrege says, "But it's not like I go around
passing myself off as Ozzy." But that's ex-
actly what he plans to do in NYC tonight—
get with some friends and hit some fancy
restaurants. Maybe even curse a little.
"You can get away with saying almost any-
thing as Ozzy," Wrege says.

He also plans to hit on Kelly Ripa. Oh
yeah.
```

I felt pretty important that morning, being in two papers. Now I had better make it to New York and do a bang-up job. I had amassed enough frequent flyer points to upgrade the ticket the *Live with Regis and Kelly* show had arranged for to first class in both directions. I couldn't remember the last time I flew first class (it might have been 1978 coming back from Graceland with Metavision) and I figured it would add the right touch of specialness to my Ozzy experience. I was totally shocked when, once seated in the front of the plane, they brought me a heavy juice glass and a tall glass champagne flute. Either of which, stomped on, would yield a serious shard that could easily be used to cut throats. "Guess they figure terrorists don't fly first class," was all I could determine. What complete confusion the airline's reaction to 9/11 had been.

I was settling in, trying to act casual like I traveled first class all the time. I was politely accepting a free pre-takeoff beer when an elderly woman parted The Curtains and started making a scene. She was demanding to be allowed to sit in first class, but only had a ticket for coach. "My son bought me this ticket, and he would never, *ever* put me in coach." The attendants were calmly trying to get her to return to her seat when the captain emerged from the cockpit. He was quickly informed of what was going on and offered her two options: sit down in coach or get off the plane. Like an idiot she chose to de-plane. How many hours must she have cost herself with that move? Our plane then sat at the gate for an additional forty minutes while the baggage guys tried to find her suitcases in the belly of the fuselage. They couldn't locate them, so after considering the security conse-quences the captain made an announcement: "Ladies and gentlemen, we apologize for the delay. We have checked the woman's identifica-tion and have confirmed it, so we are going to fly with her bags on board." Applause erupted the length of the plane. I finished another complimentary brew and shook my head. "Can't these peasants calm down?" I thought to myself, really getting into the First Class groove. The woman's bags had entered the twilight zone, and no doubt her son would be disowned by the time the airline decided to let her see them again.

After a delightful flight, (first class is very civilized I discovered—they called me "Mr. Wrege"), I was met in the Newark airport by a nice driver guy holding a sign with my name on it. This made me feel pleasantly important. He guided me across the scorching blacktop to the town car ABC had provided. In the back seat was a fresh copy of *The New York Times* and a cold bottle of spring water. I felt even more important. We were heading down the freeway when I leaned forward and bragged to the driver guy, "I'm on my way to do the *Live with Re-gis and Kelly* show. He responded, "I drove Regis once and he's a complete asshole." "Is that so?" I muttered, not caring one way or the other. While the driver launched into un-welcomed details about his run in with Regis I gazed out the window at New York's skyline, then coastline and tried to ignore him completely. I had to change the sub-ject to stop him. "Where would someone go around here to see a rock star trying not to be seen?" He listed a few spots and I wrote them on the back of my plane ticket stub that I soon misplaced. I wasn't going to be on a schedule that allowed nightlife anyway.

It was 95 degrees in New York and, not being used to humidity living my life a mile above sea level, the heavy city summer air hit me hard. The essence of the area around Times Square was pretty over-whelming. A mixture of diesel fumes, urine, fresh and rotting garbage. "It's the greatest city in the world," I reminded myself—it just doesn't smell very good. ABC was good enough to put me in a very nice hotel called the Rihgas Royal near Times Square. A two-room suite with a fine, large chocolate swirl marble bathroom. I unpacked and took my Ozzy costume inventory. Good. I hadn't forgotten anything crucial. I set it all out where I could see it, lined up and ready to put on the next morning.

I ventured out to experience Times Square and to find a deli for snacks and beer. The heat was oppressive. I was sweating a lot even though I was dressed mainly in white. The stench was horrific. Standing at a street corner waiting for the light to change the sewer gas almost overwhelmed me. It smelled like hot death. I completely lost my appetite and went back to the hotel for refuge from this hell. I called my friends Barb and Jeff to make arrangements for dinner and later waited for them in the hotel bar along with a Kid Rock look-alike who'd also been booked for the show. A dead ringer, the Kid Rock was from Florida, was a sheet metal wrangler and spoke with a very soft and quiet voice. "My kid respects me now," he said of his characterization and recent fame, and I felt a slight tug at my heart. How sad. His son likes him better now that he looks like someone famous. At dinner I tried out my character a bit on the folks inside the trendy futuristic-chino/Asian-cuisine place Barb and Jeff suggested. I was in Half-Ozzy mode, which consists of no makeup or jewelry but all black clothes, my blue granny glasses and my hair worn down. I amused a few patrons but found that New Yorkers are a tough crowd. I got the impression that the real Ozzy Osbourne wouldn't have turned heads there.

The next morning I got up at five am so I'd have time to put the gear on and do my hair before they picked us up at 7. I'd stayed out too late with Barb and Jeff and felt pretty tired. Since we were told there was going to be a makeup artist at the studio I didn't mess too much with my face, but I did put on my black eyeliner. Kid Rock was waiting in the lobby with a Pamela Anderson. A girl with bright red hair emerged from the elevator and I recognized my Kelly Osbourne. She was young and with her mother. I went up and hugged her like an old friend. "Kelly, glad to see you!" I yelled in my Ozzy voice. She was a theater student from the Midwest and her mother was obviously pushing this whole look-alike thing. "She," (pointing to her mother) "did all of this," Kelly said, "she really wanted a trip to New York." We waited in the lobby awhile for the rumored Howard Stern to show up but we were late and decided he could find his own way. (He had taken a separate car to the studio already, being a New Jersey resident.)

We were taken to the ABC building in upper Manhattan. I guess it makes sense, but when I watched television all of my life I never pictured the studios being in skyscrapers—I pictured them more as standalone studios like Hollywood, but they're stuck in the middle of office buildings. I enjoyed walking through the building making Ozzy-like mumbled comments to grins and smiles of the office workers at their desks and in their cubicles.

We were led into a conference room on an upper floor that was serving as a staging area and Green Room. Our Howard Stern was already there and bore a striking resemblance. I waited my turn for the makeup artist, sitting around eating an occasional donut. I asked the hairdresser lady to help me highlight the underside of my hair, to get the cool red flame look Ozzy has. The dye job Krish had given me back in Boulder was fading. After spending an inordinate amount of time trying to prop Pamela Anderson's hair in an acceptably curly pile on top of her head, the makeup lady took me into a little side room with a sink. She looked at the back of the rave temporary hair color with disdain. With a "harrumph!" she bent me over the sink and started spray-painting the back of my hair. I felt pretty.

With my newly sprayed locks I returned to the Green Room where Howard Stern was freaking out. "I'm a *dee*-jay," he said to the producer. "No you're not. You're a delivery guy," she insisted, "That's what you told us. We wouldn't have called you back if you would have said you were a professional entertainer. When they ask you what you do, what are you going to say?" "I'm a delivery guy," Howard said sheepishly, looking at the floor. "Right," she snapped. Man, these little producer ladies can turn tough all of a sudden.

I waited until after she'd finished berating Howard Stern then tapped her on the shoulder. "I have a long black reverend's coat like he wears or a black leather coat like I've seen him in. Which would you like me to use?" She said she wanted to check out the reference photo they were going to use for the on-screen side-by-side comparison and dispatched a production assistant to get it. He returned with a printout of Ozzy in a black leather jacket. "The jacket," she said, in one gesture handing me the printout and turning to hassle Pamela Anderson.

The look-alikes hung around the Green Room for what seemed to be a long time before we were herded downstairs to the studio. It would be a half an hour before the audience was allowed in and we were to be "blocked," or shown where we would enter, stand and exit. The *"Regis and Kelly Live"* set stretched all the way around the huge studio. A corner of it had been made to look kind of like a high-tech deejay's loft. (I felt a bit sorry for our pizza delivery Howard—he'd be sitting in a faux dee-jay booth but couldn't say he was a dee-jay. Oh the irony.) Howard was to sit behind a microphone and do a Stern bit. We were all going to come out one by one and sit on the couch after we'd spoken with Regis and Kelly. Ozzy was going to be "Howard's" first "guest" is they way they described it, which was cool because it meant I got more couch time on camera. It was odd but it felt natural to suddenly be greedy about such things as network television face time.

The producer suggested that we stay in character for the entire interview. I was disappointed that the picture they had chosen for the split-screen side-by-side shot was Ozzy with an open-mouthed menacing smile. I didn't really think it was the most Don-like of Ozzy looks I could pull off. But I wasn't about to cross the producer lady by asking if they had any other shots. The look-alikes were shown the mark on the stage to hit and we had an off-camera monitor directly in front of us so we would see the side-by-side shot as it happened. Our segment was at the tail end of the show. All of the look-alikes stood for a long time behind the flat where Regis and Kelly were making vacuous comments about the morning's headlines. I noticed a guy sleeping in one corner. "Union," I whispered a bit too loudly to Howard Stern." To my embarrassment the guy opens his eyes and shoots back, "It's not my shift," and goes back to sleep. Awkward.

I listened as Kelly Ripa introduced Howard. I was positioned just off stage waiting for my cue, sneaked a peek around the corner to check out a sliver of a view of the audience. From behind the set piece I saw Regis and Kelly's cue card being held by a grip off camera and for the first time learned our segment was called "Rock-rageous Lookalikes." "Hmmm…" I thought. "I can do something with that." My mind was racing. I got thrown by the "stay in character" direction. I had a few things I wanted to say, definitely the plug about our company for my boss, and a line about my Mom. About a week after I told her about my Ozzy situation she left me a message: "I tried to watch one of those awful shows but there was too much cussing. Why can't you just look like someone else?" I called back with, "That was your job."

But I couldn't figure out why "Ozzy" would be saying those things—staying in character was going to be weird. As I looked at the piece of masking tape at my feet that was my offstage mark, I chastised myself for not being crystal clear, just moments away from stepping into the lights of national television, about what I was going to say or how. I made a mental note that I would never allow myself to be in that position again. I was clearly panicking and knew it. I tried to get my emotions under control. I resolved, at that moment, to play The Boulder Outdoor Cinema that coming Friday night as Don Wrege, to try to get a sense of my own identity back. This Ozzy stuff was all a goof. This is not me. Have fun with this you idiot. You're taking it all too seriously!

"You're on," the producer lady said and gently pushed me forward.

I waddled onto the set in an Ozzy stumble to applause and let out a weak, "Rock and Rollllllll!!! "You've really got the walk and the whole look down," Regis said. "It's much easier to do when I'm drunk," I replied in character to a few laughs. "Why are they calling this Rock-REGIS Lookalikes?" I deadpanned. Kelly snickered, "That's good," she said, getting the joke. Regis went along with it, god love him, "No…it's Rock-RAGEOUS!" he smiled. "Oh!" I recoiled in mock surprise. We were off and running well I thought. "What do you do for a living?" Regis asked. I started to, in Ozzy's voice, describe the scene at The Kentucky Derby that had led me there, falling out of character about half-way through. I felt more comfortable with my own voice, but worried as I spoke that I was going to offend the producer lady. "You've been to Millionaire's Row right? The Kentucky Derby?" I Ozzy-stammered. Regis answered, "Sure." "Well I work for a company that does the Kentucky Derby website and I was shooting video of celebrities for the site and everyone was calling me Ozzy," "Uh huh," Regis nodded, "So I decided to have some pictures taken and I put them up on a site and it just took off from there."

"Do you dress like that every day?" Regis asked and laughing I said no. The audience laughed too and Kelly said, "Well let's do a split screen." With that my eyes locked on the large monitor they'd positioned underneath the camera's lens about four feet in front of me I did the best I could, watching the monitor carefully, to pull my lower lip into a position that better matched the Ozzy photo they'd chosen. "Yeah, that's great! Good job Don!" Regis allowed. The crowd applauded. My star turn time was over. I hadn't worked in the line about my mother's quote, but I had one last shot. As I turned to sit down on the couch noticing on the side stage monitor that the wide shot included me, I shoe-horned in one more line, "I like your Kelly better than mine," I said, and got a decent laugh out of Ms. Ripa. (Oh yeah.)

As soon as I sat down, my bit pretty much over, I started to run over in my head all the things I wanted to say and how few I'd actually gotten out. By this time Regis and Kelly were interviewing the Pamela Andersen clone. I sat there on the set, looking out at the bright lights and the audience in the bleachers, thinking about how I came out of character in such a sloppy way and began to get a bit depressed. I was so exhausted but the situation was so cool. Sitting there on the couch, on national teevee with no more responsibilities, enjoying the show from in front of the cameras, my mood evolved into a pleasant kind of sleep-deprived reverie.

They took a long commercial break during which I noticed a cameraman lining up a sweeping hand-held shot and practicing it over and over. I figured that they would come out of the commercial on his shot and I reached into my pocket to get my Stunt Dove. "Can I do this when you shoot?" I said to the cameraman, holding the dove in my mouth. "Let me check," he said and started talking into his headpiece, presumably to the director. He came back with, "Yeah, no problem," and I waited for his cue. I told Kelly, sitting next to me, to get into the shtick and pretend to admonish me if we caught the camera for any length of time. The little light on the front of his camera went on, he started to swoosh it around, I stuck the head of the Stunt Dove in my mouth. As if we'd rehearsed it, Kelly grabbed the dove from my mouth and hit me in the leg as I pulled a confused expression. It was a nice three-second bit, smoothly executed by one professional cameraman and two amateur wannabes.

I started to feel a great sense of fun and relief and was beginning to enjoy myself immensely. I also felt a kinship with my fake daughter and unconsciously placed my hand on her knee as a 'thank you' for going along with the gag. A long-held shot of this hand-on-knee pairing was broadcast and the reaction I got from most of the folks I knew who tuned in was, "You had your hand on your daughter's knee!" It was amazing to me how many people commented about this, so my standard retort became, "I can do that—I'm from Kentucky."

The show ended with the look-alikes standing in a group yelling "Sharon!" with me in the center. Kelly Ripa joined in with great gusto. Ms. Ripa struck me as totally robotic and plastic, but in a very nice way. Her smile is automatic. When she smiled and shook our hands I wondered where her head really was. Probably walking her dog or something. I guess an outward plasticity is a result of meeting so many people and doing two television shows a day. I can't imagine how she had the energy and focus to pull that off and I certainly didn't hold anything against her. But her friendly gestures, while much appreciated, might as well have been phoned in. The woman is truly amazing though if you consider the amount of work she puts in. She went from the Regis & Kelly Show to her daily soap opera. She exhibits an astounding amount of drive, energy and grace and reminded me that show business is so much harder and less glamorous than it appears.

My friends Barb and Jeff were in the audience and took a snapshot of me with Regis after the show. Regis was very nice about posing with everyone. I appreciated the fact that he took the trouble to learn how to pronounce my last name correctly. (I'd have to disagree with my town car driver's opinion of Mr. Philbin.) Before I could get a shot of myself with Kelly, the producer lady wanted us all to follow her. "We're going out on the street for some B roll (cutaway shots). "Sometimes we build little vignettes." Cool. More face time I thought. It was just as hot as the day before outside, but the streets in upper Manhattan didn't smell as bad as Time's Square, which was a relief. The look-alikes were to walk around on the sidewalks and the crew was going to get footage of people reacting to our little group of make-believe stars. This is when I *really* got a sense of exactly how dis-interested New York pedestrians can be. Like I experienced at the trendy restaurant, I don't think they would care if the REAL Ozzy walked by much less a fake. None of the look-alikes were getting very much reaction from the general public. Rimulets of eye make-up were dripping down my face. Ozzy was melting. The hairspray dye was starting to turn my sweating neck bright red. "My god, look at your neck," my fake daughter said. It looked like I'd been shot. We obvi-ously weren't getting quality footage so we wrapped up and were taken back to the hotel. The look-alikes traded email addresses. I handed out my fake Ozzy "business cards." The Kid Rock had many pictures taken standing beside the fake Pamela Anderson. No doubt his son will be impressed.

Due to concerns about New York and terrorism, I had no desire to stay around for July 4th 2002 in the Big Apple. I got home late the night of July 3rd. All the way back to Colorado I berated myself for what I thought was a poor performance and a missed opportunity. By the time I reached DIA I was absolutely distraught. The beers on the plane probably didn't help. I got home and checked my videotape machine that I had set to capture the show. In my drunken haste to pack I'd rigged it wrong and missed it. I was almost grateful because I would have been up until the wee hours of the morning watching it over and over, but was a little irritated with myself for screwing up what should be an easy recording task. I wondered for a moment if I was subconsciously sabotaging myself.

My parents and friends had taped the show for me so I figured I'd see it soon enough. The morning of the 4th, my friend Paul Bailey rang the doorbell holding a VHS dub of the broadcast. It was a nice surprise. He wanted to watch it with me but I asked him if I could watch it alone. "It's a ritual...plus I sucked." "You didn't do too bad," he said leaving me with the videocassette. I sat down to watch and was pleasantly surprised. Sure I came out of character, but got a few laughs and I looked okay. I had dragged myself through depres-sion for 24 hours for this? He was right. It wasn't half bad. I watched it over and over again.

The following day was Friday and I was scheduled to perform at The Boulder Outdoor Cinema solo. I was bone tired and generally freaked out about everything, but I had promised myself on the edge of the set in New York that I'd do it so I did. The Boulder Outdoor Cinema is run by another friend, Dave, who works with cities with pleasant summer climates to run feature films outside on weekend evenings. Boulder's outdoor theater is situated in back of the Boulder Museum of Contemporary Art and next to the Dushambe Teahouse. The landscape in the background behind the movie screen is the towering Flatiron mountain range, foothills of the Rocky Mountains. As the sun sets filtering orange through the hills, a dork in all white, starts singing to an audience in lawn chairs waiting for the darkness so the feature can begin. I turned in what I felt at the time was a lackluster performance of a set of fine sad love songs from T. Bone Burnette, Keb 'Mo and Delbert McClinton. Strumming my guitar and singing into the night with my hair pulled back in a ponytail, dressed in non-Ozzy white and wearing my regular non-tinted glasses on, I reclaimed Don. After the performance I packed my gear in Bluebell then took a half hour to stroll along Boulder's Pearl Street Mall with a brand new sense of belonging to my community. I watched the buskers performing for dollars and change and felt a kind of kinship. A couple of drunk college guys looked at me and one shouted out, "Hey Ozzy," as they passed. I had to smile. Even without all the crap on, it still happened.

4

MTV's Wannabes

"I remember when The Beatles first happened thinking 'wouldn't it be great Paul McCartney married my sister?' And here I am 36 years later singing Hey Jude with him."
- Ozzy Osbourne

As part of my research I signed up for "The Official Ozzy Osbourne Newsletter" delivered via email every month or so. Friday the second of August I received the latest edition announcing that a new MTV show was auditioning Ozzy "wannabes" this coming weekend.

```
Tryouts This Weekend! MTV's Wannabes

Requirements to tryout:

1-If you wannabe Ozzy you must LOOK between
the ages  16 - 35
2-Live within 4 hrs. driving distance from NYC
3-Be able to provide your own transportation
to the tryout, makeovers, practice, and shoot
day.


THIS WEEK!!

If you have anything in your closet that you
think makes you look like something the artist
you're trying for, wear it when you come to
the audition. It will give us an idea of what
you might look like if we pick you. If it's
Ozzy...try to find some black make-up...or
```

```
come all in black... or maybe a wig... or have
fake blood.

Ozzy Osbourne -- Get's Me Through / Crazy
Train / Mama I'm Coming Home

The audition is easy. You don't have to look
like 'em already. If you're picked, MTV will
transform you into them. You don't even have
to sing that great. When you get to the audi-
tion we'll have a CD player, and the artists
CD's with the songs listed above.

All you have to do is come to the audition and
show us you have what it takes to act like the
artist.

MTV's "Becoming Presents: Wannabe" is NOT a
karaoke or lip-sync show. It's the read deal.
No fakers or posers. Just real fans, with real
talent, who want to show the world...they got
what it takes.
```

My heart sank then leapt. It's a sign, how could I *not* do this? I'm on a roll! Omigod...they're doing this thing Sunday...that's quick...but it's on a weekend and my boss won't fire me for it. After all, I'd only miss the Monday. Hmmmm...I'm certainly no four hour drive away, and at 48 years old I was 13 years outside of their limit of "looking 35." I decided to call the producer directly and ask if I should even bother. Not reaching her directly, I left a voice message saying I was qualified in some ways, but not others...that they could check me out at my website and to give me a call if they think I should show up.

I didn't have much time to plan, in case the producer said it was a go. My friend Paul found me an online eFare for $215. This might work. I was too excited to calm down and wait for them to contact me so I left another message a couple of hours later. "MTV has al-ready kind of decided I look like Ozzy," I pitched, referencing Las Vegas photo shoot. I hung up and started to stress. Had I left too many messages?

Paul emailed me "...still available..." updates to the eFares. They were being snatched up. Time was running out—I had to make a de-cision. At around 4pm I called MTV again to find out. It was six pm New York time. This time I got a live human, the producer's assis-tant. The young guy asked, "Is there a way I could see a picture of you?" I replied, "Are you near a browser?" "Yeah." I gave him the URL, heard some tapping, then a pause, then an exclamation. "Is that YOU?" "Yeah," I answered proudly. "Well I'll show this to Lauren as soon as she gets back. They're wrapping up a shoot and she should be back in an hour and a half or so." I felt elated. It sounded like I was on board.

I was set to jet but I hadn't heard the final word from the producer. Five o'clock came and went, and returning home I started packing up my music gear to perform for The Boulder Outdoor Cinema. I thought that if the producer doesn't call, at least I'm performing tonight. This was some kind of weak self-reinforcing rationalization I was trying to run on myself to ward off any disappointment I would have to deal with when I didn't get "the call." It was also a healthy distraction. Bluebell the Love Van was fully packed up and ready to head downtown at about 6:15pm. I was dashing a last email off to my father telling him that the mission was called off when my cell phone rang.

"Hi, this is Lauren from MTV." "Oh hi, thanks for calling back," I gushed. "So you're going to be my Ozzy Sunday?" She commanded as much as asked, as only a New York girl can. "Well, sure if you don't think I'm wasting my time, I'd love to fly out." Lauren was all green lights "So see you Sunday then. Awesome!" I hung up and my heart stopped. I deleted my half-written email and called Dad with the news. To me this would be a great circular connection. Book-ending the last twenty years of my life with another MTV performance to compliment my 1981 debut. It was a good story—in my head anyway. I called Dave, the fellow who runs the Outdoor Cinema, and begged off that night's performance.

Must...buy...ticket...fast. Checking the flights online, there were still two choices out and four back. Got the phone number for The Chelsea Savoy Hotel. "To hell with the Web, I'm going to call 'em direct," I decided. Got a cold foreigner on the other end. "We only have a $145 double bed." Whatever. It was walk-able distance from the studio...I'll save money on cab fare I thought.

With my two reservations confirmed I had the destination end covered. I now had to take all of my equipment out of the Bluebell, which was slightly irritating. But only slightly because I needed a way to work off the new adrenaline rush talking to Lauren and booking the trip had triggered. Once the Love Van was back in the hangar, I made a short mental list of the stuff I had to do to get out of the house the next day. Everything had to be done before I went to sleep or I wouldn't get any. Plus I had to be up at the crack of dawn to boot. But wait...the songs!

Ozzy sings in a different key on his records than he does live. His recordings go back thirty years, and his once "high and reedy" voice isn't so high and reedy anymore. Many tunes have been moved down a step or two so he doesn't give himself a hernia trying to hit the notes. This key change situation was a great concern of mine since I couldn't sing that high either. I devised a plan wherein I would capture the audio from the Budokan DVD, (Ozzy's most recent performance I owned) via a microphone held in front of the teevee set into my mini-disc recorder. Then mix to Mac to burn a CD-ROM of two of the three songs I might be asked to perform. (Even though the email said we could choose, I was worried I would be thrown a curve ball so I wanted to be prepared.) There was no way in hell that I was ever going to be able to sing *It Gets Me Through* in the key it's in so I focused on Mama and Crazy. It was going on 8:30pm and I still wasn't packed. I printed out the lyrics. I printed out the itineraries and Lauren's email.

While I packed, I mixed and burned the CD-ROM. By the time I'd battened down the hatches it was going on 11pm and I needed my rest. Set the alarm for 5:30am so I'd have time to make sure everything was tight and I could do a full Idiot Check. Left the driveway at 6:30 or so and headed out. I felt like I had my shit together. I was getting used to this grab-and-run travel, strangely enough.

My first impression of the Chelsea Savoy was good. The neighborhood was different than Times Square, a *lot* different. It didn't take long to figure out why. It's a gay thing, and they keep the place really nice and neat. I appreciated the little gardens, greenery, flowers, clean streets and gutters, etc. If I have to put up with a couple of monstrous bikers hugging each other or a couple of over-buffed bodybuilders walking hand in hand and smooching on the street so what? I really like what they've done with the place.

The hotel room was fine. Nothing special, but clean and more than large enough with two beds to spread my Ozzy stuff around. My first task was to locate the studio where we would be shooting the next morning. I asked the cold foreign guy at the front how I might get to the address, and he said, "You can either go down this way or that." "This way or that?" We both laughed. He said you have to go in that direction (gestures) and you can get there either way around the block."

I started walking and it was hot. Even though I was in my light white pants and a white tee shirt, it was hot. Really hot. I was checking everything out on my way down 19th street and noticed the "Alcone Professional Makeup" sign hanging outside a little shop up ahead. I think to myself, "I have everything I need." Then it occurs that this shop being on my chosen route this afternoon is too much of a coincidence—I have to go in. I waited while a tattooed super-buff black guy wearing a black wife-beater tee shirt bought a tube of white and a tube of black face paint. He was with his white boy friend. "This will be fun," he giggled at his buddy. Trading racial roles for a party later, I supposed.

I told the lady behind the counter I was doing an Ozzy impersonation and described what I was planning to use in the way of eyeliner. She informed me that the powder I'd purchased at The Ritz back in Boulder was all wrong. "Ozzy doesn't sparkle," she deadpanned, "here's some flat black." She proceeded to instruct me in the fine art of brushwork and sold me a little one that looked like it was out of my Famous Artists School for Young People kit I had when I was 14. (*Famous* artists...the best kind.)

The little makeup store turned out to be right up the street from the studio where the show would be taped. When I walked up to the old converted theater, I double-checked the address, then committed the facade to visual memory and turned around to go home. I chose a different zig-zag route back to check things out. I have to give NY that much—there's a lot to see everywhere you look. I stumbled along, eyes gawking this way and that, in a sensory overload.

On the way back to the hotel I passed a sandwich board propped on the sidewalk outside the Monster Sushi bar across the street from the Chelsea Savoy, and picked up a card that read, "7pm, $7.00 - Off the Top of Our Heads Improv." One of the thoughts I'd had when I was driving Bluebell to the airport was that I'd like to see some Big City comedy if I had some time. When I'd visited some folks in New York a couple of years previous, a highpoint was seeing Robert Klein take the stage at a lower Manhattan dive. It was the Big Apple after all, these kids should be good. And conveniently located right across the street from my hotel! It was fate again. This trip might have been a good idea.

I scored a couple of cans of Bud on the way back to my room. I called Joe, the Robert De Niro look-alike I'd met in Las Vegas, and scheduled dinner for the following night. He was nice enough to meet me downtown and even offered to show me around after we ate.

I was having a problem memorizing the damn lyrics to the two Ozzy songs I was going to have in my repertoire for the next morning. I was blocking. I could feel it. How strange—when I learned songs for my Boulder Outdoor Cinema gig, remembering lyrics wasn't a problem. Now I couldn't commit to memory the simple phrases of a couple of sophomoric Ozzy Osbourne songs? I listened to them both repeatedly, *Mama I'm Coming Home* and *Crazy Train*, the night before I flew, singing along with Ozzy as I packed. But I still felt I needed practice because I couldn't get through two renditions of either tune without forgetting the words. I was freaking. I needed a beer. I wondered if the lobby bar had opened and went downstairs to find out. I found the waitress and bus boy having their early evening meal on the bar in the empty place. I took a stool at the far end with my lyric sheets. The waitress put down her fork and served me a Becks, since they didn't have Bud.

The comedy theater was just a block and a half down 23rd, on the second floor of a building squeezed in between two taller ones. One had to press the buzzer to be admitted. I was there at 7 sharp but no one answered, so I figured to hell with this and went back to my room to study Ozzy's lyrics some more. There I was in the hotel room, as the city darkened, headphones on, singing at the top of my lungs with my face pressed into a pillow folded in half lengthwise to muffle the tone. Saturday night in New York and I'm yelling into a pillow listening to an Ozzy song on my mini-disc. I did this for about a half an hour before I headed back down to the lobby bar for one more brew before trying the comedy show again.

This time the door was open. The theater was up a filthy stairwell, tiny, dimly lit and scary. Almost eight o'clock by this time, here were about thirty people seated, and all I could find was a folding chair right up front. Damn...caught. I couldn't just walk out if the show sucked. Looking around me the intuition grew that it was going to, and it did. Big Apple? Big Yawn. At some point in the performance I started jotting down notes about stuff that had happened to me that day, and I hoped they thought I was a critic writing about them. It was over an hour before a blackout to change scenes let me escape through the back curtains. I was trying to recognize some value throughout the ordeal, "I am more comfortable with performing after watching these losers..." kind of mental programming. I wasn't sure it was working.

I went to bed straightaway. But there was partying down the hall. "It's Saturday night in New York...calm down—deal," I scolded myself. I surrendered to the situation, got up and put on the headphones. I played the first minute and a half of "Mama..." and "Train..." multiple times, mouthing the words, eventually singing softly. The partying echoing down the hallway was covering any noise I made.

Throughout the night the partying noise woke me. At 2:30am, when a girl was standing outside my door talking loudly on her cell phone, I finally had to get up, pull on a pair of pants, open the door (she was almost leaning on it) and yell, "SHUT UP." At 4:30am they woke me again, a bunch of them in the hall, and I considered calling the front desk and figured fuck it. Deal. I rocked myself to sleep repeating the words to the two songs in my head. I was still forgetting the chorus.

I got my Ozzy self together in the morning. Tried out the new Alcone-bought black eye makeup and paintbrush. They both worked really well. I wore the standard issue Ozzy Adidas sweat pants, plain black long-sleeved tee shirt (to hide my tattoo-less arms) wrote "O Z Z Y" on my left knuckles, put black fingernail polish on the right pinkie and I was good to go.

This time I didn't want to walk to the studio. Even at 10am it was hotter than hell, and I was in all black carrying a heavy "reverend's coat." Luckily I got a cab within a couple of blocks. We pulled up in front of the studio right on time, and there was already a line behind red velvet ropes a block long. I climbed out of the cab and all eyes were on me. I went for it: "ROCK AND ROLLLLLLLL!" I screamed emerging from the cab. A few cheered, a few clapped but what I heard was one guy say, "It's too early in the morning, dude."

Then I saw him—a true Ozzy double. DNA match. Unbelievable. Up until now I figured I kind of owned the look, but this guy bore a frightening resemblance. I walked right up to him and said, "You look great." He flashed me his best Ozzy face, that for him included sticking out his bolted tongue. There were maybe a hundred people on line. A bunch in black clothes, some with wigs, some without but with Ozzy tee shirts...I couldn't figure out who considered themselves "contestants." I found my way to the end of the line where I encountered the second dead-on Ozzy. He was short, but his look included an excellent hair dye job that his partner, who fancied herself a Cher look-alike, had done for him. I complimented him on his hair. "I had the insides of mine dyed red," I said, "but when I brushed it, the red hair is what would come out. It freaked me." He said his was falling out too. Guess it goes with the territory. I was happy to discover that this Ozzy, who I felt looked more like Ozzy than me, couldn't sing worth a damn. With two other Ozzy's present, my strategy instantly became more focused on the singing of the song and less reliance on the look alone.

After about an hour waiting outside, a production assistant with a bullhorn announced, "Would all the Ozzy's come up here please." Crowding up to the front, I realized that there were a bunch of kids, the majority really, who had no resemblance at all to Ozzy and had gone to little to no trouble to look like him. At the time I mistakenly assumed they knew they had no chance, but showed up anyway just for fun. We were outside the theater for a good two hours in 98 degree heat, many dressed in black, as a couple of cameramen rocked miniDV cams up and down the line, asking us to act and scream like Ozzy in various scenarios. At one point a production assistant put *Crazy Train* on a boom box. The cameraman walked down the line of potential contestants singing the lyrics perfectly. When he got to me I forgot the words. "Dear god," I panicked, "The b-roll cameraman knows the song better than I do." I started to mentally beat myself up, which caused what lyrics I did remember to retreat into the recesses of my heat-addled brain.

We mugged for the camera, I got interviewed, not that they used it. A bunch of us were selected to be a line of Ozzy's walking down the street yelling "Sharon!" Shoulder to shoulder, with traffic stopped and two cameramen facing us a half a block away, the Wall of Ozzy's stumbled down the street like "Night of the Living Oz," all of us yelling "SHARON!" in unison. (They didn't use this in the show either.)

Finally after almost two hours they let us inside. Everything we did was videotaped twice and then once more for safety. They were all using MiniDV cams, that convinced me that what I thought was a "prosumer" medium is actually broadcast quality. One of the cameramen I spoke with was from Austin, Texas. He, like all the others on the crew, worked his ass off. He told me that he had appeared as an extra in on of my favorite movies, *Office Space*, at the end when the building explodes! Cool! He was famous!

The set was divided into three sections: red, blue and green draped areas, each with a camera aimed into it and a boom box. The producer instructed the 20 or so wannabes that we should line the wall in groups of eight. I wanted to get it over with so I stood up and was one of the members of the first group. I was Ozzy number 5. (This may have not been the best strategy now that I look back on it.) A production assistant ran up to Lauren telling her that someone had called from the road, had been detained, but was still trying to make it to the taping. Lauren turned back to us without comment. Groups 1, 2 and 3 went into their respective booths and the boom boxes started playing. I don't know how I ended up in the middle one but I was delighted because it had the prettiest camerawoman. She was gorgeous and her name was Joy.

Oh yes it was—Joy. I grabbed my fake dove and shoved it in my pants. I figured I'd sing "Mama" to it lovingly when the time came. Joy handed me a microphone, aimed the mini-DV camcorder at me and started to ask me questions off a list she held as I was videotaped. I answered as best I could, in my Ozzy voice, trying to be humorous. I spoke of my respect for his power ballads, especially *I Just Want You*. "It could be on *Abbey Road* or the White Album."

"I'm going to ask you to sing *Crazy Train* she read from a script taped to the tripod. Stopping her I said, "I was told we got to choose between the three...I was going to do Mama." Okay. She called a grip over. To the left and right of me, *Crazy Train* was blaring from both the red and green draped alcoves, out of sync. The grip fiddled with the boom box in our alcove and *Mamma I'm Coming Home* started. I thought. I couldn't hear it. "Can't you hear it?" Joy yelled over the din. "Can you?" I asked back. "No," she said. The grip fiddled some more. I thought I heard the intro...it was cacophony all around us and I was singing directly into a mic, looking at a gorgeous blonde while I was trying to fish the Stunt Dove out of my pants. I started stumbling on the lyrics. My mind went into self-attack mode. "Dear god...you know this shit...spit it out...get a hold of yourself..."

I sputtered and staggered through a rendition of "Mama..." on top of the noise around us. God forbid they show any of it beyond the long notes in "...I'm coming hommme!" the only note I hit correctly. After I'd done my bit I just walked around and watched. The three of us who actually looked like Ozzy figured we had it in the bag. We started to hang together in confident anticipation of being chosen the three finalists. I began to stress about the days I'd need to fly, take off, recover, etc. I found a grip who had the show date list, Aug. 7, 8, - 13, 14 or something like that. No weekends. Damn it. I'd flown myself here, at a cost of $215.00 plus tax, and bought my own Chelsea room. I couldn't afford to lose my job over the time off I'd have to take to do this thing. My stress was short-lived.

When they announced the winners, a 20 year-old Asian guy was first. That was unsettling. In fact, I thought they were doing it as a camera set up. I couldn't believe it when the skinny flat-chested host chick said, "And our second contestant..." My god, they weren't fooling? That kid doesn't look anything like..." then it dawned on me. This isn't a look-alike thing you idiot. The next finalist was a gawky kid in a fright store wig. At that point I realized that the chances were slim to none I'd have to annoy my boss about time off. The third finalist (who would go on to win) was a fellow from New Jersey who fronted an actual Ozzy sound-alike band. All of us jilted Ozzys agreed he looked just like Steve Perry of Journey. On one hand I was in shock and disappointed. On the other, I was relieved.

For some wrap-up shots they lumped us together on one side of the studio to make it look like a bigger audience for the announcement of the finalists. They lined up a shot with the host chick in between the look-alike Ozzy's (not the finalists). We were comparing knuckle tattoos for the camera. "I want one," she said. I reached into my man-purse and pulled out my marker and did her up for the next take. When it was over I walked out with the short Ozzy and his wife Cher, into the still hot sun. It was a little past three I think. As we came out of the theater a guy in Ozzy gear ran up to the door out of breath, followed by a little pissed-off woman with a grocery bag full of stuff. "Am I too late?" The doorman said he was. Poor bastard had driven all the way from Michigan and missed it. He looked almost identical to John Lennon.

I'd arranged to meet my Robert De Niro friend Joe while I was in town. He was nice enough to drive into the city and spend some time with me. Joe is such a dead-on double that he went where few look-alikes have gone: Too Far. At least that's the impression one could get from the information that made it into the press.

DE NIRO MADE ME DO IT!

Joseph Manuella, 51, a former city firefighter who strikingly resembles Robert De Niro, was arrested and charged with criminal impersonation of the movie star, De Niro's lawyer said. Manuella, of Paramus, New Jersey, a stunt double for De Niro in "The Fan" and "Great Expectations," allegedly had a Visa card under the actor's name and passed around 8"x10" glossy photos with the actor's name and forged autographs. His impersonation landed him free meals, accommodations, women, and almost a movie deal. Manuella was caught when authorities hired him to appear as a De Niro look-a-like - but instead had a limo waiting to deliver the alleged imposter directly to State Police Headquarters.

http://www.courttv.com/people/2001/1116/lookalike_ap.html

Wanting desperately to talk with Joe about his interesting look-alike past, I got the distinct impression on the phone that he didn't. I really wanted to hear his side of the story so I mentally strategized about how to draw him out. I got cleaned up and ready for dinner. I called Joe and told him I wanted to find a place that I could "mess with the tourists." Knowing exactly what I was talking about he said, "I think you'll like the Stardust Diner. It's around 47th or something." We agreed to meet there.

I asked the Savoy desk lady to help me find The Stardust Diner. She called Information and got the wrong address, but it turned out to be close. When the cab let me out I didn't see the restaurant where it was supposed to be according to the Chelsea lady's directions. I looked around and asked a horse and buggy driver parked at the curb. He pointed and showed me it was right past the *Mama Mia* sign down the block. "Thanks a lot, "I said as I reached for my wallet and pulled out a dollar. He seemed insulted by my offer of a tip for the info, pulled a face, then said, "But I'll take it."

The Stardust Diner is an establishment that feeds on the hopeful artistic talent that comes to the big city to be discovered. They gotta sing, they gotta dance, they gotta have jobs, so it might as well be one where they get to work on their show-biz skills while they sling chili. This place, a fifties diner motif, had the girls in bobby sox and long pink poodle skirts. They would toss the microphone to one another, singing to the backing tracks of oldies and standards as they delivered burgers to the tourists' tables. People started coming over to ask to take a picture of "Ozzy Osbourne" and "Robert De Niro." Joe was right. This was going to be fun.

While we ate our meal, and in between tourists' photos with us, Joe started to sound like a seminar and I was thankful for it. "Listen to tapes of your character talking when you're driving in your car. Figure out famous quotes from his show that you can drop. Always be working on your material." Joe takes this look-alike business very seriously. Not only does he do De Niro to a 't' he plays the business end just as seriously as well.

We were invited to augment at least two birthday celebrations at Ellen's, with photos and Ozzy singing "Happy Birthday" to a couple of girls in a fake drunken slur over the restaurant's PA to loud laughter and applause. After pictures were taken the father of the girls came over with two business cards, one for each of us. "If you're ever in trouble in *my* town, you just let me know." His card read: "Superior Court Judge"—he was from a small town in southern California. Joe pointed to it, looked me in the eye and in his best De Niro voice said, "See, ya nevah know!" shaking a finger in my face for emphasis. "Send that guy a signed photo tomorrow. You greet people, you do a wedding reception where you stand up and have fun with the family members—folks love this stuff," he schooled me. "If you lived in the New York area, you would have no problem bringing in a grand, fifteen-hundred a month doing this stuff nights."

Joe gave me a lot of great advice that evening about the look-alike business. His theme was "you never know." You never know who is going to have work for you, or know someone who does, or who might drop your name at the right time. Joe handed out his photo business cards at every turn. "You gotta have these," he stressed. "Well, YOU gotta have a website," I countered, since he didn't, "look what it's done for me!" He couldn't argue. Joe agreed that he needed to get online soon. I offered to help in any way I could.

I was also attracted to Mr. Manuella because of his infamy and he knew it. He was accused, booked and dragged into court for seemingly taking the whole look-alike thing a bridge too far—if all you know about the situation is what made it into the media. The backstory is quite different. Manuella was conned by a flim-flam man from Jersey who was telling people he was working on a project with the actual Robert De Niro. What Manuella didn't know, was this guy was doing deals based on this false association, and in the end used Manuella, who was falsely accused of all sorts of mischief, to shift the focus and blame. (For example, the VISA card was a gag prop that was never used to purchase anything, yet it became a piece of "evidence" the con man used against Manuella.)

As someone who spent 13 years in Los Angeles, I can assure you from personal experience that there are a lot of people in towns like LA and New York (and New Jersey) who blow smoke up asses while they steal your wallet for a living. Manuella, an honest and perhaps too trusting of a guy, constantly on the lookout for opportunities to ply his look-alike craft, was the victim of an elaborate con job. It's very complicated, very sad, and an important warning to all who would dabble in show business real or fake. There are some really bad players and one can't be too careful about whom to trust.

I was too excited to eat much at Ellens with all of the hubbub anyway. Joe and I departed for an Italian restaurant he wanted me to see. When we got there I noticed his picture on the wall. (At least I *think* it was Joe.) After a while I realized that this was his hangout, and he wanted to share it with me, and share this odd Ozzy character with them. I appreciated that.

After a couple of drinks it was about ten o'clock and we left to find Joe's car. He insisted that we had to walk past Rockefeller Center first. "Have you ever seen this before?" he asked, as I spotted the head of the big gold guy in the fountain I remembered from the movies. There were tented dinner tables where the ice skating rink is in the winter and twinkly lights all over the trees. Joe took me into the buildings to see the frescos of the working people on the walls on the main floor. The theme I picked up, as I walked through looking at the paintings, was very Industrial Revolutionary. The mural was a dramatic visual salute to the lowly workers that the bastards in the offices on the floors above were taking advantage of, the way I saw it. "See that wall right there, all that white paint? That's where sometime during the 70's, some civil rights activist got pissed off about the images of slavery and had them painted over. "That's a shame isn't it?" he lectured, "there was a story to tell there and now no one can see it."

Joe walked me past St. Patrick's Cathedral because he said I needed to see it. "That's where Jackie O used to go," he pointed out, along with, "they bury the dead cardinals in the basement." We hailed a cab and 90 cents into the ride we witnessed a taxi in front of us get T-boned by a black Lexus that ran the red. A horrible crash—car pieces flying everywhere. The cab spun 180 degrees and the Lexus ended up on the sidewalk, almost crashing through the large department store windows. The well-dressed Lexus driver got out holding his forehead and began inspecting the damage to the front of his car. Joe, as if on automatic pilot, jumped out of our cab to talk to the driver of the taxi that got hit. I figured we were in a witness situation at this point—I tried to give our driver three bucks but he was already on his way to comfort his fellow driver.

Joe was at the side of the injured cab driver asking all sorts of questions about his condition, "Are you okay? Are you hurt? Are you bleeding? You okay?" The guy was in a daze—slightly in shock but wasn't badly hurt. I found out later that Joe is not only a vet but a retired fire fighter. "You have seen more in New York in one day than most people do in years, my friend," Joe laughed. He sounds JUST like De Niro, so it was like a bizarre movie happening to me but it was real life. Our driver staying at the accident scene, Joe helped me find another cab telling the driver where to take me. I slept well.

I was a little dejected about the whole adventure when I got back to Colorado though. I had already called my boss from New York that morning with a voicemail report. "In the immortal words of Ozzy Osbourne, Mama I'm coming home. They gave it to three kids. Details later." I had misread the situation. I'd been used. They weren't looking for a 48 year-old Ozzy imitator—far from it. "*MTV's Becomings Presents: Wannabes?*" was for kids in their target demographic, just like the newsletter said. I had pimped myself into believing that I had a shot at appearing on MTV by ignoring the rules, the concept of the show (take regular fans and make them into their star of choice) and common sense. At least I'd had an interesting evening with Joe.

One of the things that stayed with me through the two New York experiences was my renewed appreciation for how truly *un*-fun the entertainment industry is. It's very hard and grueling work that looks easy and fun from the outside. That's probably why you see many of the same stars from year to year, because it's fucking hard work that few can deliver and endure. The crews work their asses off. As a "talent" you want to at the very least match the crew's energy and dedication. You want to be worthy. Any and all thoughts of this show biz stuff being a lark have been squeezed of my psyche. This is a bitch. A bitch that can be leashed and heeled, but a bitch all the same. I'm beginning to think that I wouldn't want to do anything like this for a living.

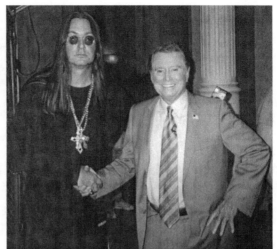

Real Celebrities I Interviewed on "Millionaires Row" at the '02 and '03 Runnings of The Kentucky Derby

View these celebrity interviews and more at:
www.myyearasozzy.com

5

The Jenny Jones Show I

*"It's kind of a fucked-up life. A rock star is supposed to say,
'Get me my Vicodins!' Or 'Run me a bath in fucking
Perrier water!' I get fucking dog shit up to the elbows and an earful of
fucking abuse."*
- Ozzy Osbourne

The *MTV's Wannabes* experience was a kind of comeuppance that I guess I needed. The whole Ozzy thing had been way too easy up to that point. My unfamiliarity with his more nuanced quirks, his song lyrics and his overall legend was humbling. I bought a book *Ozzy Knows Best, an Unauthorized Biography* at La Guardia and read it on the way back to Colorado, not that it helped much. All of the bio info was gleaned from other quickly dashed off exploitation pieces and the book held few if any revelations.

When I got back to the house there was a phone call from Peter Banks, my Austin Powers friend in Florida. He had given my name to the producer of *The Jenny Jones Show* and warned me that I might get a call. I did. Again, everything was a rush and the tape date was right around the corner. I groaned to myself that I was pushing my boss's limits with yet another trip out of town. Fernita, the producer, left a message to call her. She asked me the same questions about how long I'd been doing this, what was it like, etc. Like an idiot I interrupted her (somewhat proudly) when she said, "Well, I know you're a professional look-alike and do this for a living so we'd be willing to..." At this point I protested, "But I'm not! I have a full time job. This thing is just something I do for a laugh!" Turns out she was prepared to offer me money to do the show and I queered the deal. I was unsuccessful in numerous attempts to remind her she was going to pay me a talent fee and I ended up doing it for free. Me and my big mouth. Note to self: let people finish sentences.

I called Elyse in Palm Springs with the exciting news that I was going to be on the Jenny show. "Get AFTRA minimum at least," she advised, "then you can join. There are lots of benefits in it. That's the kind of advice you'll get from a *real* agent." Elyse was still a little miffed I had no desire to sign an exclusive representation contract with her or anyone else.

The next day I was contacted by Jim, a fast-talking, quick witted, down-to-business associate producer with *The Jenny Jones Show*. He completed the initial interview from which Jenny's on-air questions would be gleaned. He was particularly interested in the last one, which was "How has this affected your life." Without wanting to get too personal with this stranger, I hinted at my own substance abuse problems and said that if I ever met Ozzy I'd ask him for his advice on how to quit drinking. Jim focused on that. "So tell me more about that." I really didn't want to get into this on the air, and it was obvious from his insistence that Jim really wanted me to. It was standard Jenny Jones stuff apparently, get to the drinking problem right off the bat. I decided I'd stress about that when the time came, which it did soon enough.

Jim instructed me to call him every single day at 10am to "check in." Now, I'm a producer myself and I'm a worst-case scenario thinker and count myself as fairly efficient, but daily check-in calls? Turns out that *The Jenny Jones Show*, with which I was totally unfamiliar, has guests for segments such as "I Slept With My Daughter's Boyfriend," etc., and these guests can sometimes be highly volatile and somewhat unreliable. I wasn't going to disappear and check-in calls were a minor annoyance but I could understand why it was standard operating procedure.

When Jim instructed me to call him at every leg of my plane journey I began to feel sorry for him. "If I call you when I'm on the way to the airport Sunday morning that will be 5am your time," I protested. "Please call me anyway...and call me when you land in Houston, call me when you have your seat assignment for New York and please call me when you reach the baggage claim area." "You work too hard man," I said. "I know," he replied sounding exhausted.

Hi Jim,

Thanks for your diligence! I admire your dedication and efficiency too.

Here's what I have for my arrangements:

- Check in with Jim every day at 10am MST so he'll know I'm still alive

- Call Jim when departing for airport

- Leave Denver 1:10pm Sunday the 18th Continental Flight 1020V Conf. # U36GDF

- Call Jim when I get my seat assignment

- Arrive in the garden spot Cleveland at 6:01pm and proceed to get drunk

- Leave Cleveland finally at 8:30pm flight #3269V

- Call Jim with bad joke about Cleveland as I'm about to board flight with seat assignment

- Arrive 9:04pm and proceed to baggage pickup area and look for driver

- Call Jim upon arrival at Holiday Inn, 300 E. Ohio downtown - arrange for a face-to-face with Jim that evening

- Call Jim 10am Monday to check in

Hope that's all correct. $35.00 per diem gratefully acknowledged. If there's any way the show could hit me with AFTRA minimum it would be extremely cool.

If your travel office could shorten the hellish travel day by having me leave Denver earlier in the morning I'm all up for that!! Thanks for any help here.

I'm on email all day long so feel free to communi-cate that way or cell if you have any further instructions.

Thanks again Jim. Looking forward to meeting you and I'll give you folks a great performance.

Talk to you tomorrow at 10am sir!

Don
www.ozzylookalike.com

Other than again, having to get up at the ungodly hour of 3:30am the trip was uneventful. The original schedule would have put me into O'Hare at 9pm or so, and I preferred to get up earlier and get in town earlier so I could have dinner with one of the friends I have in the city. The new flight arrived at one-something in the afternoon, and as coincidence would have it, put me at the City Center Holiday Inn about three blocks from the 44th Annual Air and Water Show that was taking place at the Navy Pier. I checked in, threw my stuff in the room and headed down to the pier to join about a half a million people watch the air show. Lake Michigan stretched out on all sides, paratroopers were being dropped, gracefully circling to the ground with colorful smoky trails behind them. All kinds of military aircraft roared overhead and, of course, The Blue Angels. The blast of sound The Blue Angels passing overhead creates would be enough to convince an opposing force to drop their weapons. To my amazement they ran sorties through the city's skyline, one plane actually "threading the needle," flying sideways, zigging and zagging between several skyscrapers. "That couldn't be legal," I thought... but it was definitely impressive. I ate food from the vendors, bought beer from the booths, rocked back and forth like a white guy to the R&B group, admired the cityscape from the waterline and thought what a wonderful stroke of luck to be brought to Chicago, and particularly that part of town, in time to catch the spectacle. This was one of the parts of being a look-alike that was cool.

The next day was Monday and, as I understood it, my "walk-around" day with no responsibilities. *The Jenny Jones Show* brought me in on a Sunday, I presumed, to save money on the flight. While there were a lot of great museums to see I noticed in the tourist booklet they're all closed on Mondays. And it was raining. "Oh well, I'll find a local joint to have breakfast and read the paper." I walked a few blocks and spied a greasy spoon that served corned beef hash, that I like when I'm on the road for some reason, and went in. I thought, "Hmmm...nothing to do all day, I'll have a beer with my eggs."

Walking back to the hotel in the wet gray morning I dropped into a deli to pick up a six-pack. "Might as well make it a day," I thought. Kick back, read a couple of newspapers, watch some teevee...it had been awhile since I'd been able to relax. When I hit the room I was delighted to find a Rockies game on ESPN, and even though I'm not a big baseball fan, I found the Colorado connection a comforting one so I watched and rooted for the home team. I found an ice machine that was actually working, stuffed the six pack in the sink and propped myself up on the bed to read and watch. "A little bit of Colorado right here in Chicago" I thought as I cracked open a can of Bud Light and watched The Rockies humiliate The Braves.

I was half way through the six-pack when the phone rang. It was Jim. "We'll be over to pick you up in an hour. We're doing your vignette at 2pm." Wait a minute...I thought this was my walkaround day...no matter...I was bored. "See you then," I said and started the process of becoming Ozzy. A quick shower to do my hair, the black polish on the right pinkie nail, sweat pants, black tee shirt, leather jacket, fake jewelry, goddam eye makeup, and I decided to enhance via my rave spray, the red highlighting on the back of my hair. I tied most of my ponytail over my head, and left the underneath part out...which I stuffed into a large plastic Zip-Loc bag and aimed the red hair spray paint at the strands. "Spprrttt! spprrttt!" splattering the inside of the bag with what looked like blood—like someone committed suicide but didn't want to leave a mess. There were little spots of black eye makeup and droplets of red dye on the sink top, etc. Nothing permanently damaging, but odd. The poor maid who cleaned that room up must have thought a massacre took place.

Waiting for Jim to pick me up, I worked my way through the remaining Buds. Ozzy is, after all, easier to do when I'm drunk. Jim finally knocked on my door for our first eye-to-eye meeting. I opened it and yelled "ROCK AND ROLLLLL!" and began weaving back and forth. "You really do that well," he said of the whole package. In character I replied, "You're fucking crazy." He laughed and we were off. Passing a very disturbed family and a very confused "guest worker" cleaning rooms, we made our way to the cab for the short trip around the corner to the NBC studios. We were joined by an Eminem look-alike (16 years-old) and a Dr. Dre look-alike (18 years-old). All three of us were to have our short vignettes done that afternoon.

When we got to the studios and into the Jenny Jones Show offices I stood before a huge color portrait of her and announced (in character) "I thought Jenny Craig was fat!" to titters and muffled laughs. There were a lot of office people and production folks scurrying about. Jim, for the first time, presented me with a three page contract saying, "We'll be shooting now, but please sign this first." What? Now...I'm the grandson, son, brother and uncle of lawyers, so I'm careful about signing anything, especially when ambushed like this, then rushed. "What is this?" I had my blue glasses on, an old prescription and they didn't focus well and I was too drunk to try to make sense of the thing. "It's essentially a six-month exclusive saying you won't appear on any other television shows." Jim said, eyes on the floor. He handed me the contract that read in part:

> 3. I agree that any interview or appearance granted me by River Tower Productions is granted on an exclusive basis and that I will not appear on any other television program until six (6) months following the initial broadcast of the Program that contains my interview and/or appearance or seven (7) months from the taping of the Program, whichever last occurs.

I was astounded, but not all that surprised, then I became irritated, all in the space of a few seconds. "Jim, you and I have been talking every day at all hours for a week and a half...I've been going round and round with you people for two weeks. There has *never* been any mention of a contract or exclusive or anything. I find it quite rude that, minutes before we're supposed to tape, you thrust this thing in my face. Forget it. I'm not signing anything. Take me back to the hotel now."

I don't know if it was the beer talking or not, or whether my response would have been any different (or at least more polite) had I been stone cold sober, but there was a look of horror on Jim's face. (On the faces of the Eminem and Dr. Dre too...since they had already dutifully signed the contract without asking any questions.) "Wait just a second," he said, and fled to a back office, only to return a few moments later with a scribble in the margin of page one. "These are the only shows we're concerned about...Maury, Ricki Lake, etc." I read through the list, not having seen any of them. Then I got irritated again. "Six months may be all the longer this Ozzy craziness lasts. I'm not signing anything. Let's go back to the hotel now." I wanted another beer.

"Wait right here," and Jim was off again, only to return with some more scribbling in the margins. "Okay, how about just *these* shows until *September 13th?* That's our air-date." That I could agree to, thinking that if I did any more out of town trips before that date my boss would fire me for sure. I signed and followed Jim and the camera guy back to the producer's office, which was empty. They handed me a script that had Ozzy fumbling with a teevee remote and complaining about a dog (a stuffed toy dog on the floor next to me) pissing on the carpet. Both obvious gags from *The Osbournes* show. "No problem," I said. Once I had the general drift I didn't need to do a verbatim read.

OZZY
(seated in front of television set, fumbling with remote control)

Can't get this (BLEEP) phone to work...cost a bloody fortune! JACK!!! I wanna watch Jenny! Where's Jenny?

(Continues to fumble with remote, cussing)

BLEEP!

(Notices dog)

Princess! (BLEEP!) She's pissed on floor! I can't believe it...Sharon! SHARON!!

I nailed the scene first time. Nailed it to the wall. "We got it!" the cameraman said. "Let's do another," I requested. (What the hell, I was on a roll and really enjoying it.) "Okay, let me get another angle." We ran through it again and when we opened the door to the producer's office a crowd had gathered outside it. "You're all fucking crazy," I said in character to laughter. I wandered into a little room next door where a lady was doing offline editing. "Is that an Avid or Media 100 or something?" I asked. "Avid," she responded and I broke character to compliment her on her mastery of a system that will allow her work anywhere in the U.S. "Don't let them abuse you." She smiled. We both knew she was being abused, happy to be on a national show no matter the merit and it was the best I could do for a "hang in there," comment. I have a great respect for editors. In film school it didn't take long to figure out where the power really is, and that's in the cut.

Meanwhile Dr. Dre and one of the Eminems were being prepped for their video vignette which was to be a spoof of Eminem's video *Without Me* wherein Eminem appears in a Robin (from Batman and...) costume. Seems someone in wardrobe had screwed up, and the Eminem was trying to make it clear that the Robin Hood outfit they'd given him wasn't right. "Wrong Robin," I offered on my way out. The wardrobe lady ran past me frantic.

I was taken back to the hotel by a very angry African man who, when handed six bucks by Jim as I got in his cab started yelling, "I be here two hours and you give me this?" Tires squealed and we were away for the three-block trip. He was mumbling under his breath. He passed a line of cabs, all with drivers that looked like they came from his neighborhood and they started yelling back and forth in some strange language that reminded me of the sound of a Fela Kuti song, so I surmised they were all from Africa. When he dropped me off at the Holiday inn I handed him another five bucks saying, "Sorry they didn't treat you right." The driver snatched the bills from my fingers and squealed away in a huff. Back in the room I took the Ozzy stuff off, put some street clothes on and headed for the deli for another six. My work here, as they say, was done—at least for the day.

My supposed "walk-around" day being half work, a long hot bath seemed in order. I wanted to pre-soak the back of my hair to get as much of the red spray paint out as possible. It's really rough stuff on the follicles and I don't like seeing a bunch of hair in my brush that's fire-engine red. I lay back in a hot tub reading the Chicago version of *The Reader* and was reminded how much I miss *The Straight Dope* by Cecil Adams that they publish. I had been in stress knots for three days and this was the first time I'd felt relaxed. I sipped a cold Bud and sank into the womblike heat of the tub. Life was sweet. The plan was to meet my erstwhile film school professor Dr. Neil Holman for dinner at 6:30. He showed up at six instead with a cheerful call from the lobby as I was blow-drying my hair. I met him in the lobby with a fresh bottle of Bud in my hand and we enjoyed catching up over dinner.

By the time I got back to the room I found a voice message from Ebony, the Jenny Jones production coordinator. "We'll pick you up in the lobby at 7:45am tomorrow morning. Have all your belongings with you as you will be checking out of the hotel and not returning." Then, I checked my email. The producer for Denver radio station, 103.5FM "The Fox" confirmed that they "...wanted to do something with me" when OzzFest came to town the following week. Good lord...when will this madness taper off?

I pulled off my clothes, jumped into bed and figured I could get six or seven hours of blessed sleep before getting up at 5am to pack and prepare. I flipped on the television and channel surfed until I settled on *Rock Star* with Mark Wahlberg and Jennifer Aniston. I thought I'd seen parts of it before but didn't remember it. It is the story of a guy in a sound-alike band, so I was newly intrigued. Not to ruin it for anyone, but it turns out this "imposter," (he would correct people, "It's a *tribute...*") ends up in the actual band when the lead singer quits. The irony was delicious—here I am impersonating a rock star and might meet him Thursday in person at OzzFest, courtesy of the shock jocks. Maybe I'll...and I fell asleep with a smile on my face grateful and amused the universe had dished up some suitably ironic in-room entertainment.

I was already awake when the robotic 5am wakeup call came. My biological clock is consistent and I can't figure out how "it" knows I'm in another time zone, that I'm going to sleep at midnight have to be up at 5am. I'm lucky that my body just figures it out somehow. I had to pack up as well as dress up. I was ready when the van arrived along with three Eminem's, a Kid Rock, the Dr. Dre and a couple of other angry black rapper look-alikes I had no clue about. They had us in one of the Green Rooms from 8:10 until around 11:45. It was incredibly boring. A few donuts and some sour coffee in a pump decanter. Definitely not star treatment. I noticed immediately that there were "others" there—a father here, a mother there, a girlfriend. "Okay, we'd like to put makeup on the confronters first." Confronters? Oh oh...is this like a *Jerry Springer Show* chair throwing free-for-all show or something? By now, Jim had taken to running around with a walkie-talkie and the look-alikes had been passed to yet another associate producer who was pumping us up. "How many of you have seen the show?" Everyone's hand went up but mine. I decided to just listen. "Our audience is composed of angry unemployed people. We see a lot of them week to week. They know the only way they'll get on television is to attack you so be prepared to be attacked. If you do not look like Eminem, they will tear you apart. So go right back at 'em. Own the stage...own your character. Yes you DO look like Eminem and here's why. Shout 'em down. That's the show. If Jenny has to talk at all, you are not doing your job. Does everyone understand me?"

Good lord. What in the world have I gotten myself into? I thought it was just another star turn. I walk out, get some applause, sit down on a couch like *The Tonight Show* and have a polite discussion as Don with Jenny about how bizarre all of this is. Boy was I wrong. Then Fernita the producer, a large and imposing black woman, entered.

"I've had exactly one hour of sleep so don't anyone mess with me okay? I've been working hard to make this show a good one, you all are going to hold up your end aren't you? You're going to light up my show? I want you to light up my show. I don't want any one-word answers. If someone asks you how long you've been doing this you don't say three weeks, you DESCRIBE those three weeks. You talk. You pause we move on to the next person. Does everyone understand what I'm saying? You gonna light up my show?"

Turns out the "confronters" were just as much a part of the show as the "talent." One of the Eminems had his father there. The guy chose to wear today—to appear on national television—a tee shirt and jeans. I would not describe him as "white collar," or even "blue collar," more like "no collar." Fernita instructed him in militaristic tones, "You will attack your son. What are you going to say?" The confronter parent made some weak comments about the kid spending too much on tennis shoes. "That isn't even close," Fernita yelled. "*Attack* him, say he's driving you crazy, go *off* on him!" The father sheepishly said, "Okay." "Now! I wanna hear it now!" Fernita insisted, pulling a chair into the middle of the room. He sat down in it and she said, "Okay, now your son is obsessed with Eminem. How does that make you feel?" Suddenly inspired, the father began to rant, "He's driving me crazy, he dyes his hair, he buys expensive tennis shoes and he went to a car part store to get that stupid thing to hang around his neck!" "Yes! YES! *THAT's* more like it," Fernita exclaimed. She missed her calling—she should have been a defense attorney.

It went on like this through the Canadian Eminem's girlfriend and the mother of Dr. Dre. I began to think about what my reaction could and should be to a hostile reception. I would no longer allow myself to be in the Regis and Kelly situation of not being clear on what I was going to do as I stood at the edge of the stage. I wanted to be prepared for any eventuality. I asked the associate associate producer where Jim was. A walkie-talkie call was made and he appeared. "Jim, I'm not sure you're aware of this but Ozzy Osbourne moons every concert audience. It's kind of a trademark of his. Is it okay, if the crowd starts giving me shit, for me to drop my pants? Just to the underwear of course." Jim replied, "I don't see why not. We've seen worse." Okay then. Rehearsal.

Adjacent to the Green Room is the makeup room and a bathroom, the only bathroom we were allowed to use, which had been turned into a smoking area. The Kid Rock and the Canadian Eminem pretty much stayed in there chain smoking. There was no light in the urinal area around the corner. "Just wave it around until you hear water splashing then you know you're aimed," I said in my Ozzy voice when one guy complained.

In "The Steam Room" as I called it, due to the thick blue haze of cigarette smoke from these two idiots, I began practicing my pant pull. It's more delicate than one might think. Too fast and the whole thing might come down. I was actually thinking of my mother's feelings about my bare ass, (albeit pixelated for censor approval), appearing on national television. She wouldn't be able to tell anyone at church to watch.

Step one was confirming that I had indeed grabbed a pair of fresh and clean underwear, seeing as how there was potential nationwide exposure. Butt to the mirror, "Ahh...as white and clean as a fresh Colorado snow fall" So I proceeded to practiced the "two-thumb pull":

1 - lock left and right thumbs into sweat pants elastic at spine

2 - confirm feeling of top of underwear elastic *behind* the thumbnails

3 - slide thumbs around simultaneously, to the left and right of the tailbone area

4 - pull down and bend knees

5 - pull back up and recover

It was a delicate operation, but after a few practice pulls I was poetry in motion.

The look-alikes were ushered backstage to await our entrance. There was a collection of plastic folding chairs facing a monitor off to one side of the studio. The sound guy started hooking people up to their wireless microphones. Generally he would attached the transmitter, about the size of a pack of cigarettes, to the guest's belt in back, then run the cord and the tiny microphone up through the back of your shirt and clip it on a collar in front. When he got to me I said, "Hey, can we do something different?"

I showed him my drawer-dropping Ozzy move. I looked for a reaction and got none. He'd seen it all on this show. To allow my pants to come down, he put the transmitter into the pocket of my coat. I practiced "half-pulls" in the corner while the first group of Eminem wannabes took the stage to loud booing. "Oh oh," I thought, "These animals could get violent." At least I was prepared to "fire back," if need be.

The young Dr. Dre "look-alike," (who didn't) was next. He was verbally pummeled by the crowd, but it only seemed to give him more comedic energy. He kicked it back and forth with the "haters" and always ended up getting the punch line in. The kid was good even if he didn't look any more like Dr. Dre than I did.

When it was time for me to make my entrance, they walked me up to the second level of the set. I could hear the soundtrack from the video vignette we'd shot yesterday playing and the crowd laughing (to my relief). A floor director put his hand on my shoulder and whispered, "When I push, you go." I peeked around the set and noticed I would be running down a flight of stairs and out onto the stage. They had handed me "Princess" the stuffed dog to carry with me. I had a couple of immediate concerns. Since my blue Ozzy glasses are an old prescription, I really can't see all that well out of them. Secondly, my Doc Martin boots are big and the stairs were small—just what I don't need, to fall ass over appetite down the stairs making a bigger entrance than I had planned.

I didn't have a lot of time to worry about it as I heard the vignette end and Jenny's intro: "It looks like he took some time out from his teevee series to be here, come on out...our Ozzy!" He pushed and I went. I was ready to be booed, but to my delight and the surprise of the staff, "Ozzy" was greeted with a roar of approval. I made it down the stairs without incident, paused briefly at the base to kiss the stuffed dog, then tossed it offstage as I began screaming and running back and forth. "Rock and rolll!" "Go fucking crazy!" (which they bleeped). I really didn't have a sense of where the "center" of the stage was, but I covered all of it yelling like a loon and the audience kept cheering. "Wow," Jenny said, standing in the audience with her microphone, "Hi Ozzy!" At this point I did an Ozzy "frog leap," something he did a lot in the earlier concert days. Much like it sounds, it consists of squatting down like a frog, then leaping up as high as you can and holding your arms out in a threatening way. It's something someone dead drunk can do without falling over, which is probably why Ozzy employed its use for so many years. Thankfully, the camera was on Jenny when I did mine for it is not a graceful thing to witness.

"Oh my god it's Jenny," I said, brushing the hair out of my face, "I finally got on." Jenny laughed and said, "This is actually Don, who says he can fool just about anybody—let's do a split screen with Don and Ozzy." I looked to the monitors and saw a half and half screen with Ozzy grinning menacingly on the left, and me looking off into the distance on the right. I figured out which camera was pointing from the front, found it, and tried to pull my face into the expression Ozzy was making. The crowd cheered its approval to my great relief and delight. "God love you all!" I yelled, another Ozzy signature line, but this time I really meant it coming from me. I had heard the other look-alikes butchered by the "haters" in the audience, had been prepared by the staff to endure my own barrage of boos but instead was warmly welcomed! This was turning into big time fun.

"So what do you have to do to yourself Don, anything?" Jenny asked. "Bite the head off this dove!" I replied, pulling the Stunt Dove from my pocket and jamming the head in my mouth. I had learned from the Regis and Kelly experience not to wait if I had material—get it out fast because your time on camera will be briefer than you think.

80

I got a laugh with the dove, took it out of my mouth, improvised, "Here you go Princess..." and tossed it offstage in the same direction as I had tossed the stuffed dog.

Jenny said, "Let me show you pictures of Don as Ozzy here, see what you think," as monitors facing the audience displayed a shot that they'd taken off my Ozzy website. "Well you've got the makeup and...oh my!" Jenny said, as the shot of me in the graveyard that Marty took for the Boulder *Daily Camera* appeared. The crowd whooped its approval. "It's such a drag," I said, setting up the joke I'd waited too long to use on Regis. I definitely wanted, this time, to get the line in about how my mother was appalled and had asked me if I couldn't look like someone else instead. But Jenny interrupted me with, "You feel a connection to Ozzy don't you? You two are connected somehow, you have something in common with him?"

Uh oh, here it was. She wanted me to go into the whole drinking thing that Jim was grilling me about and I felt myself being cornered. In a sudden moment of clarity I went into a rapid-fire non-stop spiel of my own, knowing that as soon as I paused, Jenny would seize control again. "When I started doing this nonsense I bought his albums and I started looking at the show, the series—that's when it really got nuts and I just love the guy, I thought he was all about the devil and black magic and it's not true at all—he's a very positive moral soul and a great dad and just a teddy bear of a human being so I learned a lot about him." Call it a run-on sentence, but it effectively dodged her line of questioning that I determined would do nothing positive for my reputation.

My stage time expired, I sat down with the various Eminems and Kid Rock on the couch where we took questions from the audience. One guy stood up and said, "I think you people should take a look at your lives and ask yourself why you have to dress up like somebody else." I was in the middle of rebutting that comment with, "Hey, I've looked like this forever, Ozzy looks like ME!" when out of the wings came three dancing M&Ms—three production assistants in ridiculous costumes dressed up to look like pieces of M&M candy, an obvious play on the name Eminem. After that we were done.

The guests were herded into the hallways of the NBC building and handed itineraries with our information highlighted. The Dr. Dre kid was in overdrive getting right in my face with, "Man, you gonna be called back man, you killed out there! She's gonna have you back...the crowd loved you man!" I told him that if anyone deserved a callback it would be him, and why didn't he do stand up comedy? It was obvious he could think on his feet, had lots of material and could make it look spontaneous. Spirits were high all around as all of the look-alikes, even the ones who were booed had fun with it.

We were being matched up with limo drivers who were waiting outside at the curb and I was paired with the father-son Eminem team. As we were pulling away from the studio I asked the female driver, "For a twenty dollar tip could you swing by a liquor store? I want to pick up a six pack for the drive to the airport." "I hear that!" shouted Eminem's dad from the back seat. "I'd better get tall boys then, if you're involved," I cracked. The driver pulled up to the curb catty-corner from a deli with a beer sign in the window. I ran across four lanes of downtown Chicago traffic in my Ozzy getup and hustled into a convenience store staffed with Asians. I only got a few sideways glances as I left with a six pack of tallboy Buds. Eminem's father was unfortunately energized by the refreshment. So energized that when we hit the highway, he shouted, "Check this out," and emitted a long and loud fart. His kid was horrified, as was the driver and I. I clawed at the automatic window opener as the kid admonished his dad. I apologized to the chauffer and she just shook her head—she already had an extra twenty for her troubles. I pounded beer after beer, handing one to "Dad" in the backseat each time I finished one.

This time, I had brought some Wet-Naps with me so I could get the cakey makeup off my face before I got on the plane. My seat was situated next to a businesswoman who kept looking at me out of the corner of her eye. About half way through the flight I finally met her gaze head on. "Nice eyebrows," she pointed out. In my haste, and with only two moist towlettes and no mirror to work with I hadn't rubbed the eyebrow pencil off. "Why, thank you," I smiled back at her, then launched into the story of why I came to be painted that way on a flight to Denver.

82

6

The Lewis and Floorwax Show - Denver

*"If Bill Clinton can't get a blow job off his secretary
he's in the wrong job."*
- Ozzy Osbourne

Brian DeGraff, promotions director of Denver's hard rock station 103.5 FM The Fox, made good on his email promise and left me a voice message. The station wanted to "do something with me" in conjunction with the OzzFest scheduled to hit Denver August 22nd. A former girlfriend of mine is a radio personality and my first exposure to working look-alikes was a few years earlier at Denver's Great Western Stock Show. Her station had a booth there where a Dolly Parton and a Willie Nelson look-alike would pose with you for a photo. The line was half an hour long. I really couldn't believe it—the look-alikes were good, but not a *half hour* good! Everyone in line knew these two weren't real, yet they waited patiently to have their picture taken with fakes!

Excited to have a chance to get on the local airwaves, I phone tagged a message for Brian letting him know that it sounded like fun to me. The show I'd be doing was hosted by the morning team of Lewis and Floorwax, who are known to their loyal listeners as "The Masters." Along with their producer (and "Technical Virgin") Kathy Lee, they provide Denver's morning drive with a little sports talk and a lot of sophomoric shock jock humor. Dick jokes, to be precise.

I emailed Brian the next day with, "Why not a 'WIN A DATE WITH OZZY (*almost*) CONTEST'?" I hoped if they bought that concept I'd get a free night out on the town with a babe. Hey...why not? Unfortunately they didn't go for it, instead planning to take Ozzy and a couple of bodyguards in a limo to a few Denver pet stores the day of the OzzFest to shop for a dove "for tonight's show." It was the old biting the head off the dove joke, but I liked the sound of the limo.

When Brian from The Fox called me to arrange the Ozzy stunt he said, "In return for your time we can get you concert tickets for Tom Petty and Jackson Brown at Red Rocks the night before!" "Cool," I thought. If I end up with extras I can give them to my band. As it turned out, I used one of the extras to give to my boss. He'd been so patient with me taking time off that I thought he might enjoy the show and possibly meeting an actual rock legend. The radio station also wanted me to pose as Ozzy with listeners for pictures, next to the radio station promotional van outside the amphitheatre before the show.

In the late 80s I worked with Jackson on a couple of media projects back when I had a multimedia studio in Santa Monica, just up the street from his recording studio. When Browne passes through town these days I sometimes get the chance to talk with him after a show as I did this time. Jackson was playing at Red Rocks on the 19th and 21st, and Ozzy was playing the 22nd. Jackson's management kindly provided me with a couple of passes to go backstage after the show to say hello.

Tickets in hand, all I needed were my backstage passes. Red Rocks Amphitheatre is a beautiful natural rock formation turned concert venue. It has a rich history that includes the Beatles playing there in the early 60's and U2 recording their historic *Under a Blood Red Sky* video there. Red Rocks is located a little northwest of Denver and a bit south of Boulder off a treacherous stretch of rural highway 93. It's not to be driven drunk or stoned, which is irritating since concerts benefit from both.

The backstage passes are dispensed from a Will Call booth located about a half a mile down the mountain from the amphitheater itself. About 45 minutes before the show was to start I pulled up in Bluebell and waited for the passes to come down from on high. (The bands send their guest list down at the last minute, as there is a lot of shuffling of names going on.) When I saw that they were finally on the card table, with an armed police guard standing next to the fellow dispensing them, I got out of the car and reached for my wallet.

I got an unpleasant rush of bad adrenaline when I opened it and discovered I didn't have my driver's license. I knew from previous

84

experience Security would require identification before I'd be handed backstage passes. It would be one thing to talk my way around it (show a VISA card or something) if it was just a security staffer to bluff, but there was a damned cop standing right there monitoring the situation.

Earlier that day, acting on a tip from a look-alike agent I'd never met, I had gone to the main Boulder Post Office to apply for a passport renewal, since I had a possible shot (or so the agent said) at a big party overseas in Monaco. As a result of that process, my driver's license ended up this evening sitting on my kitchen table, about an hour and a half round trip drive away. I thought about it, but had agreed to do the photo thing with The Fox and didn't want to bag it for the sake of my own stupidity. But if the cop figured out I didn't have a driver's license he would be within his power and it would be within reason that he should not let me get back into my car and drive away. Or at least he could be expected to ticket me. And that particular night I didn't have the desire to have a cop go through my car. Twisted highway 93 or not, I was prepared for a concert.

In my panic I got an idea and decided to chance it. I put on a couple of my gold cross chains, changed into my blue glasses and staggered toward the booth as Ozzy. People laughed but more important, the cop laughed. I pulled out my wallet and whipped out my Ozzy card that features a picture of me in the getup and my name in bold print: "Don Wrege as Ozzy Osbourne." In my fake Ozzy voice I said, "Don Wrege on the Jackson Browne list please." It worked. They handed over my pass as they chuckled and my blood pressure returned to normal.

I found a parking place and made the mighty trek up the hill to the area where I was to meet up with The Fox 103.5 promo team at their van. I stood around for a while having pictures taken with fans and then went inside, stashing my blue glasses and gold chains and rings in my man-purse bag. Jackson opened up for Petty and did a great set as usual. I was so tired that I was thankful we would get to go backstage during the break between the sets—I wanted to go home and go to sleep. It had been a rough couple of days.

When the last chord of *Running On Empty* echoed off the cliffs, my boss and I started walking down the aisles toward the stage door. As we went, I was donning my Ozzy-ness. By the time we reached the front row I was in full-on Dress Ozzy. As we walked along the front of the crowd toward the backstage entrance, like a wave, folks started hollering and waving, "Ozzy! Hey, it's Ozzy Osbourne!" The intensity spread as we reached the stage door and it was a perfect illusion, being able to duck backstage after a couple of waves to the crowd. No one doubted I was he, not even the Red Rocks security guards.

Backstage at Red Rocks is bizarre. The whole place is built into a cliff and dressing room walls have large boulders thrusting inward from beyond the cement. The ceilings are low and the effect is like being inside of a warmly lit red cave full of musicians and hangers-on. We were led into a large room with a table of cold cuts and a few coolers with cold drinks and, thank god, beer. I was cracking one open when the security guard came up behind me and said, "Ozzy can I have an autograph?" In a replay of the Las Vegas scene, he kept insisting until I told him that I was a fake. He refused to believe it. This was a curious human reaction that I could expect from a drunk, but a totally sober security guard? Even when I come out of character? That's just nuts...but the set and setting sure supported the illusion.

When Jackson walked into the room to greet the folks I waddled over as Ozzy and his first reaction was laughter—he knew it was me. "But Don, you've always looked like this!" he said. I answered cheerfully, "Yeah, but now people fly me places. You know what though Jackson?" I lamented, "so far there haven't been any groupies associated with this act." He laughed and said, "You're probably getting *him* laid—he should be thanking you."

I was exhausted and had to get home. I didn't choose to stay for Tom Petty's set. I made the long hike down the treacherous Red Rocks Amphitheatre steps (if you have vertigo it sucks) back to the car. I could hear Petty singing, "Oh my my, oh hell yes, honey put on that party dress!" behind me in the night. More than anything, I needed sleep because I was to rise at the ungodly hour of 3am to join The Lewis & Floorwax Show in too few hours.

When I arrived at Clear Channel's Denver headquarters at 5:45am the next morning, a building inhabited entirely by various radio stations (all with synchronized station breaks), I was in costume and met outside by an intern who started laughing at the site of me. He was a large fellow, dressed in a suit. "I'm one of your bodyguards," he said. "Fucking great!" I yelled in my Ozzy voice and we took the elevator to the third floor of studios. Walking into The Fox, an engineer came out of a small voice-over booth and did a double take, almost dropping his headphones. "My god," he exclaimed, "I thought it was really Ozzy! I'm, like thinking, what's he doing up this early, or this late?"

I was led into Lewis and Floorwax's studio. The Master's (as they're called) studio is adorned with photographs of the duo with various rock stars plus an awful lot of references to penises. They aren't called shock jocks for nothing, and often the subject matter explores a kind of potty-mouth Howard Stern category. Rick Lewis, half of the morning team seemed distracted. "Where's Wax?" he asked producer/partner Kathy Lee. "He never does this... he might have hurt himself. Keep calling him." Lewis was definitely stressing out. His partner Michael "Floorwax" wasn't answering any of his phone lines, and could not be located. "He did that comedy club thing last night I think," Lewis said to Kathy. Kathy with one ear on the phone replied, "I talked to him sometime past nine." "That's late," Lewis shook his head concerned. It was approaching 6am and time to go live. I felt kind of awkward, but was imbued with a sense of responsibility to fill in whatever gap Lewis thought there was in what we were about to do.

"This is going to be brutal," Lewis said as he brushed past me walking quickly down the hall. That comment put me on notice. Lewis clearly didn't think the gag was going to work without Floorwax's counterpoint. Having been a team for twelve years, you don't get one without the other I guess. Lewis did not relish having to hold up both ends in an odd ride in a car with a total stranger. It made me aware that I had to move fast to put him at ease so that I could get as much airtime as possible and help put on a good show.

During a commercial break we all went downstairs, emerged outside and climbed into the broadcast truck right before the 6am news. Knobs were twiddled, I was given a mic as were Lewis and producer Kathy. I sat on the broadcast truck's floor, Lewis in the passenger seat and Kathy on a box behind me. We remained parked in the Clear Channel lot and soon a 25' long white stretch limousine pulled in behind our truck followed by the Fox's bright red promo van. They had decided to stay put for a while in hopes that Floorwax would show up.

Lewis starts the show. We set it up, I say a few things and on first break Lewis gives me the thumbs up like I'd done a good job. It felt great to see that. I felt I was taking some of the load off him. He was beside himself with worry about Floorwax. "I'd be pissed. I'll give him some shit when he shows up," I said, trying to bond a bit. "No, he feels bad. Whatever the problem is he'll feel bad. I just hope he hasn't hurt himself." I was touched by the concern, but I figured if Floorwax was going to sleep late I was going to go for all the airtime I could get. Lewis and I climbed into the stretch limo with the two interns dressed like security guards. The Fox had managed to find, or was just lucky enough to have, two interns who were football players or just built like it. They were in nice suits with ear pieces. In their dark glasses they were totally believable bodyguards.

Kathy Lee stayed in the broadcast truck and the rest of us climbed into the back of the double-length stretch limo. "I feel like I'm going to prom," I said. Lewis chuckled. I enjoyed cracking him up. Lewis is a professional comedian, after all. If I can make *him* laugh, I'm doing something right. Smartly dressed in a tasteful tux, sporting a waist length gray/white beard, our driver looked like a cross between Uncle Creepy and one of the guys in ZZ Top. I named him "Beelzebub" for the occasion and Lewis laughed again. The limo had a light strip running around the length of the interior that slowly changed color as it pulsated. Champagne glasses lined the walls, each with a purple paper napkin stuffed in it. Two ice compartments held beer and diet soda. I was thankful the intern pointed out the beer and I cracked one open with the help of his keychain church key. Ozzy is easier to pull off when I'm drunk, and I had a job to do.

As we drove up the morning snarl of Denver's I-25, at about 7am, an hour after the show started, Floorwax reported in. He was going to meet us at The Denver Diner on our trajectory toward The Pepsi Center and near where he lives. "Wax" had overslept after appearing at a comedy club. Floorwax is in recovery and talks about it often on the show. While it wasn't spoken, I got the impression that Lewis was just hoping nothing had pulled his partner into a backslide. It was tense and touching.

We proceeded to The Denver Diner on Colfax near I-25 in our three-vehicle caravan as Lewis chatted to the audience. I was starting to thoroughly enjoy myself in a way I'd never imagined. Definitely like being in a dream-state. Like floating on the surface of the reality, watching it unfold instead of living it. Or maybe it was sleep deprivation and the beer at 7am, but I felt just like rock star royalty and it rocked.

We pulled into the Denver Diner's parking lot with some difficulty, due to the length of the limo and the number of vehicles we had to fit in a regular restaurant parking lot. Once stopped (the stretch simply blocking numbers of parked cars, but with driver Beelzebub at the ready), Lewis said that we should just sit there a while to attract attention. How about "Ozzy has to take a piss," I offered. "Why don't we have the security guards clear the men's room, throw anybody in there out, and clear it for Ozzy to have his privacy?" I suggested, trying to be helpful, and having to piss like a racehorse myself. "Great idea," Lewis responded, to my relief.

The security guards got out of the limo and entered the restaurant while Lewis and I remained inside. By this time many heads had turned inside the diner and out of passing cars. We got the signal from the bodyguards: "all clear." Surveying the scene, I felt for believability's sake and to enhance the illusion, "Ozzy needs a security escort." I felt the star would not emerge from the limo alone in this situation. After a walkie-talkie call, one of the guys ran out to get me. He guided me out of the limo and I had him walk slightly in front of me as I Ozzy-shuffled into the diner's men's room. I pissed coffee and beer while the fake security guards watched the door from the outside. There is no better way to take a leak in my opinion. Another special moment.

When I came out of the restroom I wasn't entirely sure what to do next. "Walk around a bit," someone said, so I did. I wandered through the aisles as if confused and amazed at the same time. I spied a booth with some guys who looked like heavy metal fans so I weaved over. There was a large fellow with tattoos of demonic-looking symbols covering his neck, in a torn blue jean jacket next to a fellow wearing a wool hat too small to hide the many vertical scars on his forehead peaking out under its lip. In Ozzy's voice I said, "Nice tattoos," to the big guy and extended my hand. He shook it and looked at me sideways saying, "You're not Ozzy—I have history with the man." I went into Don Wrege Voice and said, "Yeah, I'm doing a goof with the radio station over there, nice tattoos." And I hastened back to the crew and my bodyguards. The booth full of metal guys followed. Something weird was happening and I had triggered it and it didn't feel safe.

Floorwax stuck a mic in the big guy's face saying, "And exactly how many days have you been up sir?" The big guy didn't flinch and said in an odd, guttural growl, "We've been filming a movie and we're just passing through." Floorwax asked, "Where are you guys from?" And the big guy says, "We're from DEE-troit and we're in a band." "Oh yeah?" Floorwax recoiled, "and what's it called?" "The Insane Clown Posse" the big guy said. "No way." Floorwax was stunned.

The Insane Clown Posse had a major falling out-turned-lawsuit with Sharon Osbourne over a situation where a band Sharon managed (Coal Chamber) was dropped from an ICP tour. The Insane Clown Posse is an extreme heavy metal band and I found out that the vertical scars on the big guy's friend's face were self-inflicted. He cuts himself during performances and bleeds on his clown makeup.

"What's the odds on that?" Floorwax yelled. "That the first place we'd end up The Insane Clown Posse is there, and they didn't even kill him!" "Walk around in traffic Ozzy," Lewis Suggested. Be glad to. Putting this character on, especially with convincing props like the limo/radio station promo van caravan, gives one license. The Denver Diner is at the corner of Welton Street and West Colfax Ave. I went wandering out on Welton, knocking on windshields of pretty girls' cars waiting for the light to change with, "Are you going to the concert tonight darling?" "I can't afford it." "Well," I said in Ozzy speak, "go 'round the back, tell them you know me, and they'll let you in." We'd both laugh at the absurdity at this point and the light would change and they'd drive on. All I was getting was smiles.

Suddenly one of my fake security guards, yelled, "Cop!" I looked up and sure enough, pulled up at the light at the corner was one of Denver's Finest. The stoplight had him at the front of the line. I was in the middle of two lanes of traffic harassing motorists so I started to make my way back to the limo—my safe haven. Then the cop car's public address system (sounded like the loudspeakers are underneath) barked loud enough to echo off the office building across the street, "Ozzy....Hey Ozzy Osbourne!" Everyone froze. The light changed and with that the cop drove on. It was a salute by the powers that be. The Authority. I turned toward Lewis and Floorwax, completely amazed and in my excitement and without thought yelled across the traffic lanes, "We're even foolin' the fucking *cops*." Floorwax warned,

"Calm down Ozzy," (we were on the air and had to be mindful of the FCC—luckily I was out of range of their hand held microphones). Eventually we all climbed back into the limo and the caravan started moving toward The Pepsi Center where the OzzFest was set to begin. This would be the epicenter of the gag possibilities, seeing as how there were no pet stores we could think of in the area open at 8am, so the bite-the-head-off-the-dove-riff was out.

Even at 8am there were about five hundred kids lined up outside The Pepsi Center in downtown Denver waiting to get in when the doors opened at 9:30. The outdoor carnival that accompanies the festival was setting up in back of the arena. OzzFest is a fourteen-hour ordeal. Along with a rotating list of acts, the all-day show featured such groups as System of a Down, Rob Zombie, P.O.D., Drowning Pool, Adema, Zakk Wylde's Black Label Society, Hatebreed, Meshuggah and, of course, finishing up with Ozzy himself. Among the top 25 money-making tours for 2002, only one of them was a festival and that was Sharon's Ozzfest (she runs the show) and it grossed over $24.5 million. Not bad for an aging rock warhorse and his clever wife. Not bad indeed.

Our wacky shock jock 'n' fake Ozzy caravan pulled up next to the line of fans. Our windows darkly smoked, the kids on queue couldn't see in and Lewis and Floorwax yammered on about how they were going to structure the gag. "I don't think we should reveal him on this side, this fine limousine provided by Hardbodies of Denver, I don't want to get it hurt." It was decided that pulling around the circle in front of the arena and facing outward with a lane's worth of asphalt between the borrowed limo and the possibly crazy fans was the plan. We made the turn and stopped—the broadcast truck directly behind the limo and the station's promo van behind that. All eyes were on us. The fake security guards disembarked and stood side by side at parade rest positioned a foot or so from the limo's back bumper. Lewis wasn't rushing anything, describing every detail to the listening audience.

LEWIS
Good morning it's Lewis and Floorwax, eight-twenty, twenty past eight. Alright now this is kind of a tense moment here. If you just tuned in we are, uh, we're sit-

ting at The Pepsi Center, we're parked in a limousine with smoked glass windows and we're sitting right next to a line of hundreds of people waiting to get in. We have our Ozzy look-alike with us. We, uh, man this could, this could get wild now...what we're gonna do is we're gonna have our pseudo security guys, who are huge, they got suits on they got earpieces in, they're gonna step out of the limo...

FLOORWAX
Fortunately they are big tough guys. At this point, the boys, the boys can at least get Ozzy back.

LEWIS
You guys, I mean seriously, you may have to back some people off.

SECURITY GUARD
Not a problem.

FLOORWAX
(Laughs)

LEWIS
So you guys are gonna get out of the limo, and every-body's gonna look over here, and then Ozzy is gonna pop his head out and...

WREGE
(In plain voice to security guys) I'll say: "God love you all, rock and roll."

FLOORWAX
Alright, okay...

LEWIS

So who knows what's gonna happen. Ok now we're
ready. And then we're gonna have to probably get back
in the limo and take off. Alright, the security guys are
steppin' out. Security guys are steppin' out...okay here
we go. Everybody's looking now...

WREGE
Alright?

LEWIS
Everybody's lookin.'

WREGE
(Emerging from limo) God love you all!

CROWD
(Loud screaming)

LEWIS
Alright, there you go.

WREGE
(Jumping back in limo) Get me outta here!

FLOORWAX
(Laughs)

LEWIS
Well you heard the crowd, and everybody's behaving
quite well.

FLOORWAX
They're behaving well but they were pumped! They're
all giving him the hook and horns.

LEWIS
There ya go, yeah!

FLOORWAX
They're all givin' ya the Ozzy sign I love it!

WREGE
(Laughs) I feel cheap.

FLOORWAX
No they're lovin' it man!

CROWD
(Screams)

LEWIS
Oh oh, the crowd can see 'em. The Crowd can see him
still, look there's about ten cars behind us.

FLOORWAX
We need to find a place to like, pull over right here.

WREGE
But the word has gone out, the white stretch has Ozzy
in it.

LEWIS
There's a buzz now.

WREGE
(To driver) You mean we're going back by the line?

LEWIS
Oh no, (laughs) we're going back by the line...oh
oh...okay, wonder if we should take a chance on having
you get out over there...

WREGE
I'm fine with it. Let's do it.

<STUDIO RUNS MISSION IMPOSSIBLE THEME
IN BACKGROUND>

LEWIS

They're onto this car now, they know that you're in
here. Alright now they're all lookin' at us again. We are
now, we've circled back around we're now back across
the street from the line of hundreds of fans. Alright
now Ozzy's gonna get out of the car again on the other
side. Okay. And just kind of yell at the crowd. Maybe
walk around a little bit...look at that Ozzy walk (laughs).

CROWD
(Screams)

FLOORWAX
(Giggles) Kids like him, I love it!

LEWIS
(Laughing) He's walking around, across the street! Oh
they're freakin' out. Uh, Ozzy'd better come back.

CROWD
(Screams grow louder)

FLOORWAX
Hop in Ozzy!

WREGE
I'm frightened.

FLOORWAX
(Laughs) They do love Ozzy!

LEWIS
We should get outta here now.

FLOORWAX
Okay let's blow.

LEWIS
They're gonna get pissed if they find out.

FLOORWAX
Yeah (laughs).

WREGE
I should moon 'em!

LEWIS
You wanna moon em?

WREGE
I'm up for it!

FLOORWAX
Might as well.

LEWIS
Okay, wait a minute driver, he wants to moon 'em out
that window, or out that door.

FLOORWAX
Okay I'll get out of the way, I don't want a face full of
ham 'n' eggs.

LEWIS
Alright let us sit over here...okay, and he's gonna moon
'em which is Ozzy's trademark as we leave.

WREGE
(To driver) Can I have control over this window?

LEWIS
Now does Ozzy have any tattoos on his butt or anything that they would know about?

FLOORWAX
Uh, not that I'm aware of...

LEWIS
Okay, okay here we go.

WREGE
Tell me when.

LEWIS
As we drive by. Okay driver you can go by.

I yelled at the Uncle Creepy ZZ Top Beelzebub driver guy, "Give me control of this window!" One of the shock jocks gave the 'go' and we lurched forward. I pushed the down button and the window obliged.

The vertical clearance of an automatic window on your standard 25' stretch Lincoln Town car, as it turns out, is perfect for shoving the cheeks out and, as long as the door is securely shut, provides a fine staging area for "ventilated buttocks." It is strange, that something that my whole life I didn't see myself doing, felt so natural, and was met with so much applause!

WREGE
(Sticks bare ass out window as we pass a line of several hundred fans.)

LEWIS & FLOORWAX
(Guffaws)

LEWIS
Ah yeah...(laughs) okay...

FLOORWAX
They're likin' that!

WREGE
That was authentic!

LEWIS

That's real ham there. Everybody, lookit, everybody's
salutin' ya on the way out. Ah they couldn't believe it!
They're gonna go home and tell all their friends they
were standin' in line at 8:30 in the morning and then
Ozzy pulled up...

FLOORWAX

And mooned em!

LEWIS

Ah that's great.

FLOORWAX

They'll be tellin' that story when they're eighty.

WREGE

I've now officially made an ass of myself.

LEWIS

That was great! Okay we'll take a break.

FLOORWAX

That was a classic!

LEWIS

It's Lewis and Floorwax—it's 1035 The Fox.

My ass hung out the speeding limo window for the length of several hundred devout Ozzy fans. Judging by the cheers of approval I
didn't do the brand much damage. As for the full moon, (the actual
celestial lunar equivalent coincidentally occurring over Denver that
same day/night), it was surprisingly easy. Lewis' and Floorwax's mad
cackling at the stunt made it all the more fun.
    "We're out of drive time," Lewis said during a break. "The morn-
ing just flew by," Floorwax sighed. "Yeah, if you show up at 7:15 it
does..." Lewis jabbed. Beelzebub steered the stretch back down I-25
toward the Clear Channel building. Off the air, Floorwax started
apologizing about "fucking up" and oversleeping. "I woke up and it
was light and I didn't know what day it was and I thought 'I feel great'

and then I realized..." he trailed off. I chimed in, having finished the last of the three micro-brews the limo had to offer, "I would have been pissed, but Lewis was just really concerned about you." I had the attention of both of them—looking into Wax's eyes I said, "And you'd abuse that?" Lewis chuckled. They love each other and are a truly great radio team. They are, simply, The Masters.

We shook hands goodbye in the Clear Channel parking lot. "You helped us out a lot, we should do something nice for you," Lewis offered. "Sounds like fun," I said and climbed into Bluebell the Love Van for the long ride home. I nearly fell asleep at the wheel as I cruised up I-25, but I was rolling the reality of the situation around in my head, going over what had just happened and how excited I was. Bluebell got me home again. I still had to go to OzzFest that night—this was going to be an ordeal. I pulled into my driveway at about 10:45am, too excited to go to sleep. I stomped around the house a bit trying to calm down and decided instead that I wanted to "be a part of my city." I don't know where that comes from, but when I get all excited I want to walk around downtown on the Pearl St. Mall. Dig life. It's a beautiful place for that. I changed into all white clothes (an emotional anti-black Ozzy clothes thing) and went downtown for a buffalo cheeseburger to relax.

I returned home with heavy eyelids after lunch and toyed with the notion of skipping the OzzFest entirely. I was just physically and mentally beat. But it was too important. A long nap and I should be fine. I slept until around 4pm and as I lay in bed, once again I debated the plusses and minuses of going back down to Denver (about a 40 minute drive). Better judgment won out and I dragged myself out of bed, put the black tee shirt and Adidas pants on (no jewelry) and put the blue glasses in my man-purse and headed south. (I figured I might as well have a Half Ozzy in the bag just in case.)

Bluebell's radio was already set to The Fox so when I turned it on I was surprised and thrilled to find that Lewis and Floorwax's morning show was being re-broadcast. As I threaded my way in rush hour traffic down 36 and then I-25 toward The Pepsi Center I got to relive the morning episode. I really enjoyed that a lot. There was plenty of parking and no one was trying to collect any additional money, which was nice. I'd already paid $93.00 for a single ticket to a twelve hour show and all I was going to see was the last act. I put on my blue glasses and headed out toward the front gates and pulled my hair out of a ponytail. As I approached the arena, there were small groups of people leaving and they looked at me with a curious smile.

When I got to the front gates I noticed a video crew, cameraman, soundman with a short boom and fur-covered shotgun mic, among the crowd of kids standing outside in the Smoking Area. A crew from local Channel 4 News was videotaping and a reporter was getting ready to do a bit. I walked up to him and pulled an Ozzy face and yelled, "Rock and rolll!" "Wait right there," he said, as I figured he would, and motioned to his crew. "Okay, we're going to open tight on you, you yell something then we'll pull back out to the crowd." No problem. We did a take and I was hoping to make it home before it got on the air at 11pm. Suddenly from out of the crowd, a young female appeared with a folded bed sheet and handed it to me across the security line. It was a regular white bed sheet-turned-concert banner painted in multi-color letters. In teenage girl script it said:

The Biggest, The Baddest Ozzest of all
OZZY OSBOURNE *(in his signature logo text)*
Rob Zombie
SYSTEM OF A DOWN
ADEMA P.O.D.
Where's Manson?
Drowning Pool
Long Live Heavy Metal
Rest In Peace Dove Williams, 1972-2002
Zakk Wilde's Black Label Society

I was really touched by this kind gift. The girl had put a lot of work into the sheet and I guess she was sitting somewhere she couldn't spread it out in site of the stage so she decided instead to give it to a guy who looked like Ozzy instead. It's one of my favorite souvenirs of my year as Ozzy.

It was time to find my $93 seat, unfortunately positioned right in front of a Japanese gentleman ignoring the no-smoking rule, pulling on a cigarette and vigorously blowing it in my general direction. Ozzy was preceded by a hilarious videotape displayed on the giant screen behind the main stage. Mr. Osbourne then emerged in his black tee shirt and sweat pants covered with patterned gold sequins, a large gold sequin cross on his chest, offset by upside down sequin crosses down both legs. Behind him was the drum set on a riser, and in front of the bass drum, a collection of bottles of water and what looked to be Gatorade. Next to those, open glasses of the lime green liquid, two oversized cups—one labeled "C" and the other "T." I took these initials to stand for "coffee" and "tea." There were a couple of containers that looked vaguely medical, like a prescription spray or something. It looked like the contents of a large medicine cabinet in front of the drum kit.

I bought and studied *Live and Loud* and *Budokan* on DVD to learn Ozzy's concert behaviors and stylings. So, even though I hadn't seen him in person before, at least I had a frame of reference. The man I witnessed this night was obviously miserable.

The second number in he went for the water bucket, first dipping his head in and then throwing the rest on the first few rows. He soon found the machine gun-shaped fire hoses at his feet and turned a blast or two on the audience. There was no smile on his face when he hosed the crowd—my first clue he wasn't enjoying it. He only sprayed the concert-goers once or twice, as if getting an obligatory part of the act over with. Through the binoculars I'd brought, I was trained on Ozzy and his movements. For some reason which began to seem like spite, he aimed the hose time and time again at a single bald security guy right down front. I would like to think that there was a reason for it. I just found it strange he continued to soak this poor bastard down, and it was his job to stand there to keep people from jumping up on stage. Ozzy never cracked a smile. In between each number he would turn around to "the shelf" and drink things. The two cups were replaced within the first four numbers. Trooper that he is, he did a few Frog Jumps. He jumped up and down. He didn't run around a lot, but he ran around enough. I began to feel profoundly sorry for him. And then he'd grab the hose and soak the poor bald security bastard again. It was weird. And Ozzy never smiled.

"I'd like to dedicate this next number...to my lovely wife Sharon...who's sick in hospital with ass cancer." Ozzy's image was being displayed on two video projection screens flanking the stage. I could only watch about six numbers before I started getting really depressed. Ozzy was clearly not into it. He was reading the lyrics from large monitors at his feet, singing the songs, doing the act. But he was obviously just going through the motions and I wasn't enjoying watching it so I left. I have no insights other than to say the merchandising was weak, and I found a patron's complaint on the way out to be significant. "They took my disposable camera, then they took my choker chain man, saying that neither one was allowed in, but they're selling 'em both on the inside! That's not right man." I agreed.

Bluebell got me home as I tried not to think about how sad Ozzy had seemed on stage.

7

The Jenny Jones Show II

*"The real fact of the matter is
sometimes I look at this TV show and I feel sad."*
- Ozzy Osbourne

I didn't bother answering my land line on Labor Day. Who would be calling me on a holiday, I wondered, having already spoken with my family the day before. Then I heard the cell phone ring. It was Ian, a Jenny Jones producer. "Somebody saw something they liked," he said mysteriously, "and we'd like to have you back on the show. Can you fly the 5th for an appearance on the 6th?"

I was sort of stunned. I'd done *The Jenny Jones Show* only weeks before, and they wanted me back this soon? I listened to the message again thinking it was a saved one from the previous show's arrangements. It was indeed, new. The flattering nature of the message ("Someone saw something they liked,") intrigued me. I called Ian back. "Hi, this is the Ozzy guy from Boulder. Did you just call?" Ian indicated that he had, that Jenny wanted to do a vignette with me, that this was rare, and I should feel honored. "The Jenn, huh? Well I guess I am. Sure. I'll do it." I immediately began to stress out about the date. It was a Thursday and a Friday. I had three more vacation days left and this would eat two of them, and the notice was so short it wasn't like I was going to be able to gracefully build it into my work schedule or break it to my boss in a positive way.

I told my boss what Ian had told me—that Jenny had requested this, and that Ozzy would have an expanded role in the show. I wouldn't just run on with a lot of other look-alikes. This time I would "counsel troubled youth in The Love Lounge." How could I pass that up? He just looked at me sideways. I was risking my job for this nonsense.

I had to pack that night for the early flight the next morning. I'd gotten it down to a science, made easier by the fact my dining room table was now dedicated to the Ozzy crap I dragged along. My makeup kit, the jewelry, my reference photos, etc. were all splayed out where I could perform a quick visual inventory. While I filled the suitcase, I listened to Ozzy's interview with Greta Van Susteren from a recent television appearance so I could internalize his vocal intonations, phrasing and accent.

His appearance on Fox's *On the Record* show was timely and controversial. It seems that Ozzy's management (read: Sharon?) had signed an exclusive with Barbara Walters for an interview in which Ozzy would address his concerns and sorrows surrounding Sharon's colon cancer. The original purpose of Van Susteren's interview was that Ozzy was one of many performers commenting on Elvis Presley's influence on their music, on the anniversary of his death. Well Greta threw him a curveball question, "How's Sharon doing," and Ozzy began to clutch, then sob. Being no fool, she kept up the line of questioning, drawing him out and filling an entire half hour with the very material promised exclusively to Walters and another network. I read about it on The Drudge Report website the morning before, and there were legal actions threatened if the show ran. Van Susteren chose to go ahead anyway, and I thought, "This guy stays in the headlines even when it's by complete accident!"

The Jenny Jones Show staff booked me on ATA. I had never heard of, much less flown ATA before. Their signage looked like it was a party airline (palm trees, etc.) specializing in Club Med-type destinations. It turns out that they are a refreshing relief from the shambles United has become. I was impressed with their efficiency and flexibility. This time I asked Ian to help me avoid the 6:40am flight out of DIA. If Jenny wanted me to take an additional day off work to provide her with free entertainment the day before, then this is what I asked of them. He got me off the ground at 8am with a direct flight so I'd be in Chicago in plenty of time to shoot the Jenny vignette after her second show (they tape two a day).

I was met at the airport by a friendly driver in cool shades holding up a notebook with my name written in large block letters on the inside cover. I wanted to ask him for it as a souvenir, but decided against it because I didn't want to come off like a dork, even to a driver. When my bag came down the carousel he reached for it but I grabbed it first. "I've got it dude, you just keep the car on the road." He smiled. When we got to the hotel I asked him if he had a ten for a twenty (I like to tip on the road) and he didn't. I apologized for the four ones I gave him and he thanked me with a smile.

The Chicago Hampton Inn has a kind of faux Frank Lloyd Wright lobby, with rectangular designs in the wood and wallpaper reminiscent of Wright's work. I liked it. It was about half past noon when I arrived. "Your room is not ready." Great. I had to get in costume and be at the NBC building immediately and I couldn't take a shower, shave or do my hair. I called Ian who went into high gear. "I'll call the management. If you aren't in a room in twenty minutes call me back." I walked over to the diner that's off the lobby and ordered a Budweiser. Twenty minutes later I checked with the front desk. Still no room. Called Ian…he kept me on the phone while he spoke again with the manager. The producer of the segment came on to read me the script of the vignette. "You're fooling around with a cell phone that you can't get to work, you've lost the guests for the show and Jenny is mad at you. You're both swearing and we'll beep that out. We'll have a stuffed dog and you notice it has pissed on the carpet (do they only have two jokes for Ozzy's character?) and Jenny yells at you again."

"Why can't it be a real dog?" I pleaded. "Last time they had a stuffed dog. Doesn't anyone have a shitsu?" She said, "Wait a minute," and put me on hold for a while. "Ian's mom has a little dog. She's bringing it." "Very cool!" I yelled, glad that I had pushed it a bit. She continued in a businesslike tone, "Then you go looking for the guests, find them, and talk with them a bit. Do you think you can handle that?" "No problem," I said, "sounds like fun." Ian came back on the line. "I'm moving you to the Hilton if they can't get you in the room in fifteen minutes. Call me."

I went back to the diner for another Bud. I liked the place, I was already there, and I found the diner pleasantly accommodating. A nice lady at the counter was telling me where the best music in Chicago could be found (Kingston, Chicago Blues, etc.) and even comp'd me a Bud when I told her why I was there. Her name was Jenny too, and she was a writer. "You're in my story now," I told her. With the threat of me moving to the Hilton the management magically got me into a room. The lady at the front desk handed me my "Jenny Envelope." As soon as I was in my room I opened it. There was a welcome note with the rules and regulations, a pre-paid phone card and an itinerary. I noticed that my flight out the next day was 8pm and freaked. I called ATA and was informed there was a 2:40pm flight but that was the only other option for Denver.

My god…I'm going to be sitting at Midway for five hours? I called Ian. "I'm in my room, everything's great but this flight out tomorrow is insane!" "What? What do they have you on?" I gave him the details and told him of the option. "If you can get me out of there as soon as we wrap I might be able to make it." "I'll make that my first priority!" he said. "I'll get you out of there right after the taping." Jenny works her people hard and Ian's tone of voice and assuredness made me feel like at least there was a chance.

"What time do we shoot today?" I asked, "there's no use in my sitting around a green room for an hour if I can use that time to look more like Ozzy." "We shoot at 3pm," he said, which was plenty of time for me to transform myself. "Great. I'll call you as soon as I'm dressed," and headed back to the diner for another Bud that I brought back up to the room. Once I was suitably Ozzy'd out, I gave Ian a call and he dispatched an assistant to fetch me. I shuffled from my room into the diner one last time not for a beer, but to wave at Jenny the counter lady. She laughed at my transformation. The whole place turned around and looked. I gave her the thumbs up and shuffled back out to a buzz of booths.

I was led into the NBC building once again and up to the Jenny Jones offices. Soon I was joined by some of the other guests being readied to shoot their own vignettes (mine was the only one that included Jenny herself). I got bored and lay back on the couch in the reception area. Ian's mom showed up with a little dog on a leash. The precious little thing was named Remy "Like the liquor," Ian's mom proudly told me. I proceeded to bond with it by making high-pitched whining "dog in trouble" sounds and it worked. Luckily, Remy enjoyed licking my face, which is an Ozzy-dog thing. I hoped I could get her to do the same on camera.

An older black gentleman came in with a young girl. He wore a sports jersey with "Muhammad" on it. "Does that stand for Ali?" I asked him. "Yes." I told him I was a huge Ali fan, being a Louisville, Kentucky boy myself, and having had the honor to have shaken Ali's hand once. "My daughter's gonna be a star," he said. "I'm investing a lot of money to produce her studio sessions." Oh oh, I thought, hoping she could actually sing. "I'm an ASCAP writer publisher," I started, "…and spent 13 years in LA trying to break into the music business and one thing I learned is that you should be using someone else's money, not your own." "Yeah, I know," he said. "I'm working on that," he said quietly.

The Jenny Jones Show has an odd format. It's mindless fun and involves low-life confrontations between the audience and guests. In between are comedic video vignettes that feature the guests. Unlike my previous Jenny Jones experience with producer Jim, this particular show seemed kind of disjointed, with decisions being made on the spot and the producer Natalie, although authoritative in her voice, haplessly hurried and seemingly only slightly organized.

But at this point I was drunk and didn't really care. I'd done this before and Ozzy is truly easier to do with a buzz on. I was just riding with it. Natalie handed me a script with my parts highlighted and it was pretty much what she described on the phone. I read over it and knew it would be no problem. At around 3pm I was lead into the inner sanctum of Jenny Jones' dressing room. It was a suite of rooms actually—quite a step-up from the other office environments and fit for a star. Jenny was in her personal dressing room at the end of the suite's hall, attended to by two flitting and flaming makeup men dabbing her face and brushing her hair.

The room was lit with stage lights but there was no camera crew in sight. Jenny was pissed. "If we don't do this now forget it. I'm leaving. I have homework to do and these things always take forever!" she snapped. Natalie ran out in a panic. I stood there shocked. I took a chance and addressed her directly in my normal voice. "I have to say that these kids work their asses off for you," Jenny turned to me softened, smiled and said, "Oh, I know, but if I don't blow up this will take forever. It's always like this." Commenting on one of the gay makeup men's outfit, which included a large fringed wrap draped around his neck, "Does he always wear a tablecloth?" I quipped. The makeup guy ignored me but Jenny shot back, "Oh shut up you…you Ozzy wannabe!" We laughed. The makeup guys didn't.

The camera crew finally entered. "I thought we were going to have boom mics!" Jenny yelled. Natalie disappeared again. The cameraman began lining up his shots. The soundman with the twin boom showed up at the same time the little dog was brought in. Natalie ran through the script with me. "Jenny yells at Ozzy because he's lost the guests. Ozzy is confused. He is playing with the dog. Jenny hands him a microphone. He doesn't know what it is. Jenny yells at him. Ozzy leaves to search for the guests. He says, 'Is she always this bitchy on a bad hair day? You give someone a talk show and she thinks she's the Queen of Talk! Well I'm the Prince of Fucking Darkness!'"

They assured Jenny and me that our cussing would be bleeped out. It was more authentic to have us go ahead and say the curse words and then cover them later. Ozzy "finds" the guests in the green room, confronts each and moons one. The guy says, "I have a secret crush on a girl with the nicest, hardest ass…" at which point Ozzy says, "Have you seen my ass?" bending over and exposing his crack. I was up for the task. What the hell. *The Lewis and Floorwax Show* had been a great mooning ice breaker for me. I didn't particularly like the guest I was going to moon anyway. When the vignette was finally shown on the air, this brief scene was flickered in high contrast black and white so as to render it inoffensive. Except to my mother, of course.

By the time I was put in another cab, with another south African driver who was pissed about the six dollar standard fare to the hotel three blocks away, it was dinner time. I went to the room and showered Ozzy off, put on some comfortable clothes and went downstairs to the diner for dinner. "I can't put your beer on the Jenny Jones food tab so I'll run that separate," the alarmingly pretty waitress said. "Fine." While I ate I read The *Chicago Tribune* for the first time and was knocked out by it. I buy the Sunday *New York Times* each week, and lived with The *Los Angeles Times* for a decade, but up until this point had not read a copy of The *Chicago Tribune*. It's a great paper I learned, over a salad and some meat with brown sauce.

I got to the room with a beer to go around 8pm dead tired. There was a message for me, much like before. A production assistant leaving the "We'll pick you up at 7:45am so have your things with you and be ready to check out," message. "I'll deal with Ian in the morning about the return flight," I thought, as I sat in bed. I turned on the teevee, killed the beer and woke up a couple of hours later still dressed. I brushed my teeth and then settled back in bed for some needed prep rest. I figured if I got up at 6am, I could deal with my email, pack and get Ozzy'd by 7:45 without too much trouble.

The next morning the production assistant was right on time and assembled us in the lobby. She called "Smoke," (a professional wrestler who looks like a professional wrestler called "The Rock.") waking him up. "Ian said they didn't need us until 9—I'm still in bed," he told her. "Well that's true," she reassured him, "Ian did mention 9…but I left a message last night about the 7:45 checkout." (I was slightly pissed—I could have used the extra sleep myself). We were told to meet again in the lobby at 8:45. Having breakfast in the diner to pass the time made sense.

It was going on 8am and I was dressed in my Ozzy blacks: sweat pants, black shirt, and black leather coat. My left hand was tattooed and my right had a black fingernail. When the waitress came to the booth I explained my appearance, "I'm doing Jenny Jones today as Ozzy." She replied, "Hey, a couple of people were saying that Ozzy was in here yesterday but it was you! That's a riot!" I ordered scrambled eggs, corn beef hash and four beers. The waitress asked, "Four beers? Sir, are you okay?' "Sure," I replied calmly, "I'm just getting ready for work."

I made it back out to the lobby at 8:40 to greet Smoke and the production assistant. We checked in at the studio and were taken to the green room. There are a lot of green rooms. This one was the "northwest" green room. Smoke and I weren't there long when another production assistant, a small but well built screamingly gay man came crashing through the door. "This has been the *worst* day of my life," he emoted. "I missed the train because I went to the McDonalds, (huff!) but I didn't even get the McDonald's because the line was too long and by the time I went back to the station the train just blew by (huff!) missed it by SECONDS! (huff!) and I just had my performance review and it's just the *worst* day I've ever had." He collapsed into the chair by the door.

"Well, all that changes right now," I offered in a weak attempt at support. He smiled. The door opened. A large woman holding a clipboard leaned her head in, looked directly at the emotionally crushed production assistant and snapped, "You're crap! You…are…crap! You know that don't you? You're crap!" and slammed the door.

"See?" he said looking at me apparently about to cry, "It's been that kind of day." I was beginning to wonder why people put up with this kind of abuse just to be in "show business." His new assignment was to make sure none of us left the room and he wasn't about to screw it up. Being a Jenny Jones guest obviously represents a huge flight risk.

The door swung open again and four women walked in. Now, words fail me here because "women" don't really do these gorgeous specimens justice. I looked up at Smoke. "I love show business," I said. "Damn right," he whispered out of the side of his mouth. A dark Latino tall girl with huge tits, a dazed, tall, black woman and a shorter more, shall we say, "accentuated" black woman and a lily white girl in pig tails with a short black skirt and English accent named Lyndsy. Lyndsy squealed in a lovely cockney accent, "Oh my god, my husband is the biggest Ozzy fan, he'd die if I called him and said I was doing the show with Ozzy."

"Well then why don't you?" I slurred in the best British accent I could do. She pulled out her cell phone and called him. "Darling? You won't believe this. Guess who I'm doing the show with…Ozzy…Ozzy fucking Osbourne! Yeah! He's right here!" She handed me the phone. I said, "Hello, how arya?" in my Ozzy voice. "You've got a loovely wife ya know…here she is," handing the phone back to Lyndsy". "Isn't it?" she said after a pause," "Okay…love you," hanging up.

"Oh my god he bought it!" she said. The whole room was laughing. "I'll bet he's calling all his friends right now." I offered, "You might want to call him back right now because you know he's going to be pissed." "Yeah," she agreed, you're right." She called him back. He was pissed. I asked Lyndsy if my accent was right. She said, "Say something." I did the standards, "You're fucking crazy!" etc., and she laughed saying, "You do…you do sound like him!" I took that as the highest compliment. I mean, her being English and all. Of course, I'd listened to the damned mini-disc of his voice all the way there, and the night I was packing…pushing his intonation and phrasing into my head. I was happy that even drunk, I could easily conjure an Ozzy sound and get passing marks from a limey.

The theme of this show was "I Have A Secret Crush," which made me feel a little uncomfortable since it was this type of show that ended in a murder trial. In fact, it was because of a Jenny Jones program that a guy ended up murdering a buddy of his. Back in 1996 a fellow named Scott Amedure appeared on Jenny Jones' show and told the world that he had a homosexual crush on a one 26 year-old Jonathan Schmitz. This did not sit well with Mr. Schmitz and he proceeded to purchase a 12-guage shotgun and pumped two shells into Mr. Amedure's heart, just to make a point.

This was undoubtedly the genesis for some of the wording in the Jenny Jones Show contract I was required to sign before we taped (*emphasis theirs*):

> 5. I understand and acknowledge that I may experience one or more surprises (e.g., a secret or other unknown fact may be revealed to me) in connection with my appearance on the program.

> **7....I further understand and acknowledge that River Tower Productions cannot control, and is not responsible for what happens or is alleged to have happened between myself and any person on the Program, whether such events occur before, during or after the Program.**

The guest-turned-shotgun-assassin ended up being pronounced guilty in two separate trials and was awarded 25-50 years in prison for his post Jenny Jones outburst. Since I was neither gay nor a homicidal maniac I felt I could ride out anything the show had to offer as a surprise.

There were four couples involved with our show. The drill was that either the boy or the girl who had the crush on the other, came out first and professed his or her love. It had the stench of a set-up, in that the pairs were oddly out of whack, generally one person had a performing skill and the other was a dweeb. No doubt a lot of Jenny's guests simply take advantage of the themes to get a free trip to Chicago and a little stardom on national television.

We were finally led out to the back of the set in the dark recesses behind the scenery. This time around, things seemed a lot more chaotic. Decisions were being made on the fly. There were a ton of details, props and people to move around. It was tense and busy. Standing next to a two-story cage filled with every kind of prop imaginable, we were brought a small monitor so we could watch what was going on out front. The makeup lady came by. I got on my knees and asked her to make me pale. She dabbed at me with a brush. I had already done my eyebrows and put on a bit of foundation. I was getting pretty good at this makeup thing.

I was waiting backstage when they ran the Ozzy vignette with Jenny we'd taped the day before. I kneeled down and watched, but was mainly concerned with how the crowd was going to react. There was a loud reaction when Ozzy, in the vignette, referred to Jenny as "bitchy." It underscored how contentious this show's audience is by design. Everything is a fight. I'm suddenly depressed by the base nature of this "I'm gonna kick your ass," level of behavior and emotional response to life this show caters to.

For this show, the props included three foot long pieces of foam rubber sushi, a giant road sign, and a ballerina's costume. When my pre-taped vignette was nearing its end I was steered behind the set pieces over to a door that opened onto the stage. As I stood waiting to emerge, a production assistant told me to "go center stage immediately." Center stage? I had no idea... The door flew open and I ran out screaming. There was a ramp and only one way to go. People from the audience thrust their hands out toward me and I ran along the line slapping as many hands as I could.

"Jenny, it's good to see you again," I said when I stopped running back and forth. "Ozzy will be waiting in The Love Lounge for the contestants," she told the audience while I stood center stage basking in the klieg lights. "Do you think you can find your way over to The Love Lounge Ozzy?" Jenny admonished me (for not moving) and I loped over to the couch stage right, where I was to remain for the rest of the show.

The girls from the Green Room were assigned to carry appropriate props out at the designated moment, and to stand next to three on-stage monitors with large cardboard hearts revealing when appropriate the logos: "I Want To Get Busy," "I Want To Kissy" and "I'm Sick And Dizzy." An incredibly skinny black girl came out to profess her love for her secret crush. She gushed about how hot he was, warning all the girls in the audience to "Forget it, he's all mine!" Random members of the audience waved their supplied "True Boo" signs enthusiastically. The fellow who was the clueless secret crush was then led onto the stage, after the skinny girl was led off.

He was a nice looking guy, smiling widely, and he positioned himself on a couch center stage. Jenny spoke as usual, from the audience. "So do you have any idea who your Secret Crush is?" "No," the young man said, "In fact, I don't know why they would have a problem just picking up the phone ya know?" the audience laughed, "I hope she's no monster or nuthin'." "Let's start with some clues," Jenny shouted, as the British model, dressed like Heidi with pigtails, came out of the wings holding the three-foot piece of foam rubber sushi. "Sushi! Does that ring a bell?" The young man shook his head 'no.' "How about this?" Jenny cued, as the black model walked out on stage with the huge street sign that read "35ᵗʰ and Main." "Nope," the young man indicated, pleasantly confused. A third "clue" emerged from the wings. It was the gay production assistant from the dressing room, who'd been given a dressing down earlier in the day, was now in high spirits all dressed up like a pink ballerina, prancing about the stage. As with the previous clues, this one didn't connect either and Jenny blasted right past it.

The skinny girl was brought out and the young man recognized and hugged her. She then proceeded to rap to him, a hip-hop pledge of undying love. The young man pronounced that he was ready to get busy, at which point the model holding the cardboard heart over the "Let's Get Busy" monitor removed it with a practiced flourish. Once their bit was over they were directed over to The Love Lounge, where I sat microphone in hand. As we went to commercials they would zoom in on me and I was directed to interact with the crusher and crushee. Almost all of my banter was edited out in the final aired show and replaced with teasers for another show called *Street Smarts*. (When I found this out it played a big part in my decision not to do a third Jenny.)

One interchange they did leave in was a line fed to me by producer Fernita. She ran out of the wings during one of the breaks and said Jenny was going to ask me something about Kelly, and I should answer "a veterinarian." We came out of the break and Jenny turned to me, sitting on the couch with the contestants, "Ozzy, what kind of fellow would you like your daughter Kelly to eventually marry?" I was fed one line but I wanted to go for more. "Kelly, I, I, I love her more than life itself," I stammered in my Ozzy voice. "I hope she marries a doctor because I'm falling apart," [laughter] "I'm old...maybe a veterinarian who could fix the dogs so they won't [bleep!] all over the floor." That was my big moment in The Love Lounge.

This wore on for what seemed to be a long time. I was tired. Not only was I coming down from my morning drunk but I was mentally calculating the time it would take, from the end of the show, to get me to the airport. And, I had frankly had it with this low-ball entertainment. While it was fun to get exposure, the fact that I had to point friends and family at a show so incredibly insipid took the edge off the "accomplishment." By the end of the second show I was through with it for good.

I had a singular vision when I came off that stage and that was to get the hell out of the building and into a vehicle and be on my way to the airport as fast as possible, otherwise I'd have the pleasure of sitting in Midway for five hours. To hell with that. Ian guided me around the dark backstage area into the hallway, put me in a town car driven to my absolute delight, the same driver who picked me up two days before. "Can you get me to the airport really fast?" I asked. He nodded. I figured that fate had given me another opportunity to tip the man what he deserved.

I told him that I needed to get to the airport as quickly as possible and, god luv him, he drove like a bat out of hell. Through accident scenes and heavily congested highways he ran two red lights, passed a cop car, squeezed between vehicles on both sides at high speeds. He was going for it. I remembered in a flash that putting the large, metal, sharp-edged crosses in my carry-on was a bad idea. The sharp-edged goth ring alone would get me searched in all cavities. I decided to put all of the Ozzy jewelry in the suitcase before checking in and when we hit the curb at the terminal I grabbed my bag, handed the driver a twenty (in addition to the fare Ian had paid in advance), put my suitcase down on the sidewalk, opened it and started stuffing the plastic bags with "gold" jewelry in then closing it, locking it and proceeded inside.

At this point of course I am still in stage makeup. My face is powdered and pale, my eyebrows dark pencil brown, my knuckles spelling Ozzy and my right pinkie black. Going through the highest security the government can muster in stage paint and sweatpants. On the left and right of me people are being pulled aside for "secondary screening." Not Ozzy. I just don't set those bells off I guess, and what a surprise. I'm beginning to think it's racial profiling and Ozzy is in the green zone. Old ladies are being asked to remove their orthopedic shoes and here's a man with heavy stage makeup on, nail polish, knuckle tattoo, looking like a satanic rock singer. Wave him through!

I was astounded when I got a voicemail from *The Jenny Jones Show* just a week after we'd taped the second show. "Can you be here next Wednesday?" I couldn't believe it. On one hand I was flattered. On the other hand, the way Ozzy was shoe-horned into the "Secret Crush" program didn't make any sense and I felt one of the desperate producers had run out of ideas. Plus, having done the show twice I wanted to move on. Been there, done that, know the drill, thanks a lot. I called him back to politely but firmly decline the offer. "What if we paid you a hundred dollars." I had to laugh. "My hourly rate is a hundred and fifty, and I've already taken two vacation days to perform for you folks for free, so I think I'll pass on this one, but thanks for thinking of me!" The producer was persistent. "Let me call you back in a few minutes, okay?" "Whatever."

Ten minutes later the phone rang and it was the producer with an offer of $250, then $350. "Look," I said, "I'm not trying to bargain with you, and this isn't about money." "We're busy at work right now and my boss will kill me if I take another weekday off for the Ozzy foolishness, so I think my main focus should be on keeping my job." "Can I call you back in a few minutes?" the producer pleaded. "Sure, what the hell." It rang again in five and he had his final offer: "We'll fly both you and your boss to Chicago. We'll set him up in an empty office with a phone and a high-speed data line so he can work while you're on stage. $400 you guys can split or you can give to him, and the usual per diem arrangement." I had to decline. Thanks but no thanks—I'd had enough of daytime teevee.

Then he finally got smart. Almost as an afterthought he said, "Well, do you know any other Ozzys that might be able to make it?" After a little hesitation (the competitive spirit in me) I said, "There's Bob-Ozzy in Florida, but he doesn't like to fly. Maybe he'd drive up there for ya," and with that I gave him the contact info. Hanging up I realized that I would never hear from *The Jenny Jones Show* again, since Bob-Ozzy was retired and had nothing else better to do. This ended up mattering little since the long-running show (12 seasons) was cancelled a few months after this conversation.

8

The Reel Awards – Hollywood

"I'm getting a star with my name on it put on
Hollywood Boulevard. So from 14 Landsdown Rd., Birmingham, my
name on a star on Hollywood Boulevard—
that isn't half bad is it?"
- Ozzy Osbourne

The Reel Awards is an annual charity bash that features a bunch of look-alikes giving each other prizes. It's a rather insular event but seems like an excuse for some downtown Hollywood publicity and a chance to do something nice for a good cause.

I spent 13 years in Los Angeles between '76 and '89. It had been way too long since I'd seen my LA friends, some from SIU's film school and some from my various business dealings out there. I used this as a partial excuse to sign up for The Reel Awards, buying a $250 ticket via a donation to Debbie Reynold's "The Thalians" (they donate to mental health programs). I paid in advance. The event's program hinted of Debbie's presence and an after-event rooftop cocktail party (neither of which happened as it turned out). When I booked it I thought it would be fun to meet her. I did a Web search on "Debbie Reynolds" and was impressed to find a very well thought-out and constructed Web presence all her own. The old gal still does weekly online chats with her fans. THAT's a true celebrity.

As the day approached I found myself not really looking forward as much to the whole Ozzy thing. I was more interested in figuring out how many of my buddies I could visit while I was out there in the little time I had. I was landing the evening of the event—something I started to stress about almost as soon as I confirmed my online reservation through Expedia, the Microsoft travel site. Would I have enough time for a complete costume/makeup transformation? Heck...I need at least 45 minutes! At the same time I bought my airline ticket I made car and hotel reservations. I used Expedia for this as well. I was delighted to discover that Enterprise had a car rental desk right next to the West Hollywood Ramada where I was staying. I'd cab from the airport to save the time and rent my care there.

As luck would have it, the second heaviest snowfall in Denver's recorded history of such things, happened three days before I was to leave for LA.

> DENVER (AP) A powerful blizzard paralyzed
> Colorado's capital and Front Range on
> Wednesday, closing government offices,
> businesses, schools and interstates with
> hip-deep snow.
>
> Denver International Airport was shut
> down, stranding about 1,000 travelers, and
> a seam in the tent-like roof began to tear
> under the weight of the snow. Governor
> Bill Owens and officials in suburban cit-
> ies warned residents to stay home unless
> travel was absolutely necessary.
>
> Owens' spokesman, Dan Hopkins, said the
> storm may be the worst to hit metropolitan
> Denver in 20 years.

A total of 35 inches of fast-falling, wet and heavy snow ranging from two to four feet depending on where you were in the greater Denver area brought the city to a standstill. The airport, our billion and a half dollar "all-weather airport, the "airport that never closes," was rendered impassable. Pena Boulevard, the only thoroughfare into and out of the airport, was closed down. People were trapped in their cars. Roofs were falling under the snow's weight all over town. Electricity was out. My main concerns were, "Will I be able to, a) get out of here, and b) get my money back if I can't?

I put a call into the organizer of the event and left a message asking if I couldn't get there, could she cut me a break (since the $250 was both a donation and a ticket to an event). I didn't get an answer. So I figured that much was gone. I called my brother, who is a road warrior traveling four or five days out of every week, for advice. He put the fear in me about "these new ticket deals" like one gets online wherein if the flight goes and you aren't on it, you have forfeited the entire ticket price.

Snowed in at home on Tuesday, two days before I was to depart, I turned to the phones and the Internet. The phones were useless ("...because of high call volume, please place your call another time..." that message played for two and a half days). While I could get no human being to confirm one way or the other that my flight was on or off, the flight was still showing up on United's website even though the airport from which it was to depart (Washington) was completely closed. Wednesday morning Colorado's governor Bill Owens ordered citizens to remain in their homes and off the streets except in the case of emergency. The next day, my flight day, I awoke to the news that the state capital was shut down as was the post office and most businesses.

Denver International Airport came to a screeching slushy halt the previous Tuesday afternoon. Over a thousand trapped passengers fought over territory on the airport terminal floor for their families to sleep. The tremendous amount of wet show caused DIA's distinctive multi-million dollar fabric roof over the Main Hall to rip under the heavy load. Everyone was evacuated and pushed outward toward the booking desks. There was simply not enough room and the conditions were dangerously overcrowded, but there was nowhere else to go.

The outlying parking lots had closed due to eight foot drifts and no way to bulldoze the cars out since they couldn't get a bulldozer in to do it. Interstate 70 was closed from where Tower Road meets Pena Blvd. through Morrison, Colorado and sections of I-70 would remain closed for the next 48 hours. Denver and the surrounding areas had been brought to a standstill—square miles of blue-white silence.

My ticket was for a 1:30pm Wednesday departure. By working all Tuesday night on the runways the DIA crews had two cleared, and that was enough for United to fly some of the 80 planes out that were trapped by the storm. They flew out empty. The thousand trapped passengers were very unhappy about this. Denver is a United hub and United had to get the planes back into the system—a system that had been severely disrupted by two days plus of trapped plane downtime. Putting random people onto unscheduled flights, trying to find bags, etc., would have been a nightmare, if it could have been possible at all. But tell that to someone who knows a plane is going to Chicago and they've slept on the floor with their family and are just waiting to get back to Chicago. The business logic doesn't fly, so to speak, with that particular passenger.

Booking travel arrangements online can be a wonderful, cost and time saving thing. Until that is, you want to change something out of the ordinary. On that frantic Tuesday I was trying to plan in advance for the worst case scenario and running into the new world of "Customer Relationship Management." Expedia.com's "customer service" took me to the edge of my patience. When I called the 800 number, first I "spoke" with a pleasant male robot voice—a very professionally soothing voice. After spending a few minutes with him I wanted to kill something.

> Robot Voice: "Please state your itinerary number, or ask for help."
>
> Don: "Uh..."
>
> Robot Voice: "Please state your itinerary number, or ask for help."
>
> Don: 1608657...
>
> Robot Voice: "Excuse me while I find your records."
> "This won't be a moment,"

I guess I should be thankful that they didn't have music in the background, but they effectively redefined "moment." All I was able to get out of the system was a confirmation of what was already on my reservation, nothing else.

By the second call I was trying to figure out when "he" was going to let ME ask a question, which was never. I finally discovered how to get through to a human being and that's when my blood pressure went up. After a long wait (WITH music this time) I was shunted to some phone farm that I suspected was going to be offshore. I guessed India and I guessed wrong.

Human: "Herro, mayh ah herp roo?"

Don: "I just spoke with the Ramada and they said if I didn't arrive by Thursday, that even though I'll be charged for that night as a cancellation penalty they'll cancel the entire reservation, that includes Friday and Saturday night which I might be able to make, United willing. Unless they hear from Expedia I'll lose the entire thing. I need to know the procedure to get you folks to fax them this change."

Human: "Whah?"

Don: "Only Expedia can hold onto my room for me in case I'm late. How do I do that."

Human: "Do roo mine iffa I puh yoo on hole?"

Don: (sigh) "Not at all."

It went on for a very long and fruitless time, during which I discovered the primary purpose of this "customer service" was to frustrate you enough that you'll just give up and go away. After being no help whatsoever, but finally wearing me out:

Human: "Iz thare annithin erse ah cudda herp roo wif?"

Don: "Yeah, I'm snowed in here in Denver. What city are you in?"

Human: (unintelligible)

Don: "Did you say 'Asia?'"

Human: "Ah in Manirra..." (giggles)

...at which point I think a blood vessel burst somewhere on the left side of my brain.

On the morning of my flight it was announced that DIA would open for what was described as, "no incoming flights and only a few outgoing flights" at 10am. Since I was departing at 1:30 I felt at least I had a chance. United's website indicated that the Washington leg of my flight was cancelled, but the Denver to Los Angeles leg was still departing on time. Thankfully, the plane I was on was one of the planes trapped at DIA they had to get back in the system.

Wednesday morning the sun was finally out and the streets in Boulder started to clear. The major thoroughfares were open and it was obvious I'd be able to at least make it out to DIA, about an hour away from Boulder. I didn't know where I might park, but I felt the need to protect my $330 investment in the ticket. If my brother was right, I stay—it goes—I lose. I figured if Pena's closing had trapped Denver-area residents in the parking structure their ability to leave Wednesday would free up some spaces, so I'd look there first. At worst I'd give myself enough time to hit one of the outlying hotels that might have shuttle access.

Bluebell got me out to DIA and as I drove in, the three green "OPEN" lights above the two covered parking garages gave me my first feelings of hope. I drove past the uncovered lots, noticing how most of the cars were solidly blocked in by snow. That sucks. There were a few spaces on the northwest-most corner of the west garage and I claimed one with glee. "This might just work," I thought as I dragged my bag behind me toward the main terminal building.

When I got to DIA's second floor via the parking garage elevator, it opened onto a scene the likes of which I've only seen in war movies. Red Cross blankets with families strewn on them. Some had used the blankets as makeshift hammocks, tying both ends to payphones. Entire families tucked into corners, huddled on the floor. A sea of people standing hollow-eyed, roped into lines snaking back and forth, waiting to speak to someone, anyone, from the airlines. I entered at the far end of the terminal and became more and more disturbed as I walked past this humanity, packed stacked and miserable. The feeling, the mood hanging in the air was electric, dark and contagious. I felt my face grow flushed for no reason. "Oh great, I'm having a fucking stroke."

I was inside the building by about 10:20am for a 1:30pm flight. Initially, I thought this was enough time, and I wouldn't have been allowed onto Pena Boulevard before 10am anyway, so I was doing the best I could schedule-wise. I found a group of people who looked like they were part of a line that, according to the lit-up sign, was for "CONFIRMED FLIGHTS BETWEEN 11:45AM AND 1PM." From the number of people in front of me it was obvious that I wasn't going to make it up there within the hour, so my 1:30pm departure time would serve me well the closer to the ticketing desks I got. I thought.

There was only a handful of ticket agents on duty. I grumbled loudly to no one in particular but to everyone within earshot, that United surely knew what the situation was out here and to have a skeleton crew dealing with it was unconscionable. "93 of their employees didn't report to work today," I was informed by a voice in the crowd. Turns out that no one could get into or out of the employee parking lot anyway. It was just a mess, and it got worse.

A brave little United lady with a clipboard was fighting her way through the crowd, trying to be helpful while looking increasingly desperate. "Okay people listen up...if you were booked on a flight before 12:30 you have missed your flights. Please step out of this line and get in that one over there that says: 'REBOOK'." "I've been in this line for eight hours," a guy only a few people in front of me yelled at her (which disturbed me for a lot of reasons all at once), "I'm not getting out of it." "Me neither," someone else shouted. "We're getting up to the counter!" a third voice cried. It was getting ugly. Suddenly people who hadn't seen a United employee close up for too long a time could vent. The little lady steeled herself. "If you get to that ticket counter and your flight has already left, they will not rebook you—they will tell you to get in that line over there." Having made her point, she ducked into a sea of bags and bellies and disappeared.

No one moved.

I was beginning to panic. I started asking people around me which line I was in. There was such a mass of people you couldn't really tell which way the zig-zag pattern was pointing without getting out of position, which was something instinct told me not to do.

I asked folks standing around me what time their flight left. "12:30" a couple in front of me said, "But didn't that lady just say that you should be in that line over there?" I asked. "We're not moving. We've been here all night." I felt a really bad feeling in my stomach. I felt myself grow beet red. It was now 12:30, I had been there two hours, not moved at all, and those in front of me had no chance to better their situation—only make mine worse. "Excuse me," whispered a tall quiet man with a sled full of bags, "Did you say you were going to Los Angeles?" "Flight 373?" "Yes," I replied, immediately hoping this man would tell me I was in the right line and that everything was okay.

"We're never going to make it."

His voice grew soft, but urgent. "Unless we skip over diagonally through these people and muscle our way to the ticket counter we won't get on that plane." He was right. I was faced, not for long, but faced with a karmic dilemma. Should I ignore the rules, butt in line, violate common decency just to save three hundred dollars on a ticket, justify two hundred and fifty on a donation and eighty-nine on the hotel room reservation? "Can't we just kind of, get in that line over there? It seems to be shorter," I pleaded sheepishly. "That's because the guy at the ticket desk is dead slow. Have you noticed? This lady here has done twenty in the time it takes that guy to do one."

This person, whoever he was, was right. He was also right about butting in line. By now the decision made itself, as all semblance of polite society vaporized as people suddenly blew the queue to rush the ticket desks en masse. The velvet ropes were unhooked or just knocked to the floor with the surge forward. I'd never really seen anything like it at an airport. Luckily for me and my new friend, (the devil on my left shoulder as it were), the guy right in front of us had his arm in a splint and a cast on his leg. Poor bastard, probably came to Colorado to ski and have fun. Instead he broke his bones and has been forced to sleep in pain at the airport for two days. "Get out of my way," was my only thought. At this point it was pure survival instinct. All it took was the tall man behind me to egg me on and convince me I was doomed otherwise.

"Lead with your shoulder," he whispered close to my head. We pushed the broken man aside easily and oozed through the crowd. To my amazement people let us. I'm big enough at 6' 2" and the quiet man even taller. Once we had momentum we shoved our way toward the ticket desk, the quite man dragging a bag cart that left a small human wake behind it.

It had become a mob scene. When the crush of people reached the desk with the efficient woman manning it, I was two layers of frantic humans back. The quiet man was holding onto my shoulder, "Tell her party of two," he said. I waved my ticket over my head. Others thrust their tickets into her face causing her at one point to say, "Push that thing any closer to my nose and I'll tear it in half." (Probably going outside of the United Customer Relations handbook for that comment.) I stayed focused on her eyes and in the brief moment they met mine, I sent her a psychic "I'm pitiful" glance and moved the ticket over my head two inches in her direction, but still keeping it within my personal space. She reached out and grabbed it. "Party of two," I said, as the quiet man's ticket slid under my arm and onto her desk.

I did not look backwards. I couldn't. I was afraid. I didn't take any photos of the people who had spent two days there, who were standing in line. I just wanted away from it. The horrible truth about the business of travel is that planes are far more important than people, and while this made sense to me, it didn't make it all right. The first ones in aren't the first ones out. A thousand people on standby and I'm going through security while they watch. Eyes down. Walk fast. The terminal building was deserted. I went immediately to the gate, with 20 minutes to spare. I got in line. The quiet man said, "Hey, lets go get something to eat, you've got a boarding pass you're okay."

"I'm not getting out of this line," I said, "until they tell me I'm in the right one, and then I'm going to sit right here until they let me on the plane." He looked at me like I was crazy and others must have felt the same way. This strange beet-red, pony-tailed man checking in twice just to make sure and locking his gaze on the jet way door. I couldn't believe we'd made it. The quiet man and I had bonded on a severe adrenal level. He later sent me a book he'd written. I gave him advice on his website.

Our plane was going to hit the ground at 3pm and the Reel Award's "Red Carpet Entrance" began at 6pm. I hadn't left myself a lot of time to waste getting from Los Angeles International (LAX) to the Ramada, turn myself into Ozzy and then cab to the theater. I had booked my room at the West Hollywood Ramada partly due to its proximity to my friends' houses and the Henry Fonda Theater, and partly because the hotel is steeped in rock and roll history. Known for many years as The Tropicana, superstar groups and struggling new-comers alike would bunk there between performances and parties (sometimes indistinguishable events). Thanks to its central location just off of Sunset Strip, and its low nightly rates, such stars as The New York Dolls, Johnny Cash, Blondie, Iggy and the Stooges, Dennis Hopper would wander in and out, and Tom Waits lived at the hotel for quite a while. Until 1987 it was the scene of untold debauchery, then it began its transition into the scene of untold debauchery of another kind that it is today.

Santa Monica, especially around the area where The West Hollywood Ramada is located, is a gay bastion. Like the Chelsea neighborhood in New York, they keep the place nice and neat. The LA locals call the area "Boy's Town." Twenty years after I'd lived in Santa Monica, it was interesting to see the transformation. Booking through Expedia I got a pretty good deal. I found out that Expedia usually has the less desirable and therefore cheaper rooms in its inventory. My room at The Tropicana was nice enough of a layout but looked out over an access alley filled with dumpsters where nightly drug dealing and illicit sex acts take place. Neither of these bother me as much as the trash bin trucks backing into said alley at horribly early hours of the morning.

I saved twenty bucks a night on my room and got to listen to the beep-beep-beep, clash and clang of the alley's dumpsters outside my window. Little matter. I had to make it to the Henry Fonda Theater within the hour. I threw on my Ozzy gear, drew the letters O-Z-Z-Y on my knuckles in what now was an automatic process, circled my eyes with darkness and called a cab.

Arriving at the theater, I was delighted to find a bunch of look-alikes I knew; a lot of people from the press; a red carpet; video crews and stretch limos. Bob De Niro emerged from the crowd with a bunch of Ozzy CDs. "These, my friend, these are for you. You...you're good you." Bob pointed out that we could make multiple entrances for the cameras. Once we emerged from the car and strolled down the red carpet, we just ran around the block and got back in the limo queue again. This De Niro guy works every angle. We climbed back in a limo for the second time around, along with Ed Sullivan, and Bob said, "Freeze, let me get a shot of this and I will send it to you."

The evening's event was nice enough. The organizer had a lot of photographers running around taking pictures, then triggering their strobe flashes repeatedly to give the impression that a *lot* of actual photos were being taken. The best Whoopi Goldberg I'd ever seen was at the podium introducing the Lucille Ball when a morbidly obese Elvis, who had been around since the red carpet entrance, stood up in the back of the hall and began screaming loudly and incoherently. The Drunk Elvis! He was soon surrounded by security and escorted out.

After everyone calmed down, several veteran look-alikes plus bonus star *Laugh-In* veteran Joanne Worley (filling in for Debbie) came out and did routines. Then Rich Little, the main event of the evening, did about twenty minutes of voice impersonations. He was fabulous. I wish I could have shaken his hand but he left the hall quickly after his astonishing multi-character routine soaked up the applause.

Video cameras on cranes whooshed overhead. I decided to get drunk—it had been a stressful day. Austin Powers joined me. We were promised a cocktail reception on the roof, but this didn't happen. We were standing around in the lobby after the show wondering what to do when Anna Nicole yelled, "We're going to The Rainbow, who's coming with us?" I held up my hand and lurched forward.

In 1978 when I lived in Yorba Linda, California I would sometimes make a special trip into Los Angeles, about 45 miles west. The Roxy nightclub is a relatively tiny venue that more often than not served as a record label showcase. Back in the late 70s and 80s when I was occasionally lucky enough to score a ticket, I saw the likes of Todd Rundgren and Captain Beefheart from about four feet away. Next door to the Roxy there's a restaurant/bar called The Rainbow, its walls plastered with photos of famous rock stars. When I was an aspiring star myself, visiting The Rainbow was like taking a hike to Rock Mecca. For a kid from Kentucky, sitting on a stool that an actual rock star sat on when he got shitfaced, was for me a religious experience.

So when Anna Nicole announced that The Rainbow was the party destination, I was right there with her. A car pulled up in front of the theater and we jumped in. The driver looked vaguely familiar, but his orange hair was throwing me off. "You know me," he mentioned as we pulled away. All I could see was the back of his head and a slit of his eyes in the rear view mirror but I figured it out. "The Imperial Palace!" I shouted. It was Dan Gore, the producer responsible for putting me on stage for my first appearance a year earlier at Elyse's 2nd Annual Celebrity Impersonators Convention.

Tony Soprano, Robert De Niro, Anna Nicole Smith, Austin Powers, and Ozzy pulled into the Rainbow's lot. Dan left the car with the valet and we piled out like circus clowns, walking into smiles and open arms. Robert De Niro began working the Italian-looking manager. "You...you have a gift you!" We were shown special tables right up front, ringside on Sunset Blvd., We ordered tasty unhealthy food. There was a chill in the night air but The Rainbow had heaters lining the outside wall, and mushroom like propane trees providing waves of warmth.

Tourists passing by on their way to the Roxy would do double takes, then stop and ask for pictures with us. One drunk came over and addressed the entire table, passing out single sheets of hotel room note-pad paper with the Playboy bunny logo on it. "I'm, like, working with, you know, Playboy 'n' everything up at the mansion you know? A party of look-alikes would be grea..." "Hey," Elyse stood up interrupting him. Shoving her card in the guy's face over the heads of the look-alikes she said, "If you want to contact anyone here, go through me."

This didn't sit well with Austin Powers who, in his crushed velvet suit was baking beneath the heating elements. Sweating and flushed he said to the guy, "You can contact me directly," handing the Playboy note-pad guy his own business card. Elyse scowled. It was an awkward moment but it passed quickly. Anna Nicole had brought along a beautiful young lady, introduced as her "new manager." I gave this new manager my own Ozzy promo pack as an example of what I think any look-alike should have on hand. It included printouts describing each of the major events I'd done plus a CD of my on-air incident with the shock jocks at Denver's OzzFest.

We partied and ate until well after 1am. Elyse, her fiancé Howard and I shared a cab back to the Ramada. Howard seems to be about 70 years old and Elyse and he had just announced their engagement. (You go boy!) When we arrived back at our hotel he says, "Where's the bar, d'you want a drink?" At that hour I was about to run out of gas, but here's this old coot ready to party some more. I told him that he was my hero and we went searching finding nothing open. But we tried. I liked my new friend Howard. Best to get some sleep though because the next night I was going to party hard with my old friends from film school and I was really looking forward to it.

I hadn't seen them in way too many years. Could be ten, could be fifteen, it had been too long. I set aside time to get together with a group that included my buddy Richard Whitley, whom we call "Whit," an actual Hollywood screenwriter whose hits include the classic *Rock and Roll High School* with The Ramones. When I called him that evening Whit said, "Giermo insists we have to go to see The Thai Elvis." "What's that?" I wondered. "Never mind," he said, "it's all arranged."

The group gathered, partied a bit then drove for what seemed like a long time, finally pulling into a crowded parking lot. I fell out of the car to see an otherwise normal neighborhood restaurant, except there seemed to be a whole lot of people wandering around in front. Giermo must have arranged a reservation because we got in, leaving a parking lot full of hopefulls behind.

Hollywood's Own Thai Elvis
Kim Adelman's The Girls' Guide To Elvis

It's become a kitchy local girls night out thing to go to Palms Thai Restaurant in Hollywood to catch Thai Elvis, a.k.a. Kavee Thongprecha, who performs weekends only.

Believe it or not, he sounds a lot like Elvis.

And the restaurant recently got voted on of LA's top 75 restaurants by the Los Angeles Times.

```
Go when you're in LA (you won't be
disappointed):

The Palms Thai Restaurant
5273 Hollywood Blvd.
(323) 462-5073
```

From what I could tell, The Thai Elvis' family staffs and runs the joint. We were situated in our booth when a hush came over the place. The Thai Elvis, an elderly man who looks to be nearing 60, strode to his position at the karaoke control panel—one leg cocked, the other locked. The mirror ball started spinning, the colored spot came on, and The Thai Elvis leaned into the microphone, raised his right hand and "Rove me tendel, rove me tloo." wafted over the crowd to rapt attention.

What is absurd, is actually beautiful here. And it's appreciated. The Thai Elvis is obviously a true fan of the music, and doing the best he can to interpret it. The crowd, otherwise cynical and soured by LA hipness, finds this bizarre scene somehow real, in a sea of bullshit, here's a guy who simply likes Elvis, loves to sing, owns a restaurant, has a captive audience and hey...suddenly the sullen crowd senses humanity. There were even some goths there, maybe finding out what being alive is all about. The food sure wasn't the draw.

I let the others order for me. I had decided to party my ass off. I hadn't seen these guys for so long, and we used to party stupid back in Carbondale, so I was going to revisit that lack of common sense for an evening. Others were driving. A plate of Thai food was placed before me and I tore at it. I was attracted to a small bright green chili pepper on the condiment tray and popped it in my mouth. What followed was intense pain followed by brain chemistry to counteract it. I popped another. This hurt like hell, but I'm suddenly very happy. I have tears running down my cheeks, but I have a new love for the entire human race. There's something in these green bullets that...I think I'll have another one, HOLY SHIT! ....ow...oh, okay, I see everything clearly now. Who needs drugs with these things around?

I'm tripping out on these peppers and The Thai Elvis' daughter walks up to me wanting to have a picture taken. I'm honored in a way, and saddened in another, because I got the impression (she didn't speak English) that she may have thought I was the actual Ozzy. Our party went back to Whit's house, and into his garage that he's converted into a writer's den. More drinking, more smoking, somehow I made it back to my hotel room thanks to my film school buddies. Fade to black.

The next morning I had it all planned out. Plenty of time for a nice early breakfast on the terrace facing an empty Santa Monica Boulevard, return the rental car right afterwards then grab a cab to LAX. I didn't want to be rushed so I gave myself plenty of time. Things were proceeding nicely, breakfast down, rental car returned, last idiot check of the hotel room to make sure I didn't forget my Ozzy glasses or anything and the cab was on the way. Watching what's left of Los Angeles pass by as we whizzed the back roads on the way to the airport ("Faster than freeway," my foreign driver said), I compared what I saw with the LA I remembered from the 80s. I made the right decision to get out when I did.

I flew in on United and I told the driver to drop me at their gate. There was no curbside check-in so I got in the long line to check my bag and read the paper as we inched forward. The line was extremely slow and I was happy I'd given myself the extra hour that I had. About thirty minutes later I got close enough that a United lady was looking at people's tickets right before they were called to the counter. "This isn't a United ticket," she said looking at mine. My stomach fell through my feet. "What?" "Look, it says right here, Alaska Airlines." What the fuck? My return trip to Denver had been brokered to a puddle jumper. "Where's the right terminal?" I asked, slightly panicked. "The other side," she pointed out the windows.

The terminal at Los Angeles International is a huge loop. I was, say, at 3pm and the proper terminal was at 9. I dragged my bag, heart pounding now, and started to walk it—my second mistake. It was taking forever, but once I started it seemed crazy to flag a cab or something to go a quarter of a mile around the circle. I staggered up to the Alaska Airlines terminal, now sweaty and red-faced. This time I sought out an airline employee so I could make sure I was in the right place. I wasn't. I couldn't believe it either...it was like the Twilight Zone all of a sudden. Sure, it SAYS Alaska Airlines, but it's serviced by American. Of course, their terminal is (you guessed it) next to United's, back at 3 o'clock. Okay, no time to walk it...it's down to the wire. I cursed myself for my stupidity. How could I eat all of my spare time like this? Not reading the ticket carefully enough! What an idiot.

I ran outside and flagged down a shuttle driver. "Can you take me around to the other side?" pulling a five dollar bill out of my wallet. He waived the cash away and said, "Jump in." After all my careful planning to have plenty of time I made it to my gate with only fifteen minutes to spare. Thankfully there was a bar directly across from it.

Still rattled from my brush with my own travel incompetence, the three beers at the Travel Point Lounge only giving me an uncomfortable feeling of helplessness, I sat in an aisle seat, pulled out my reading material (which included a *New York Times* and a Lyndon Laruche *Special Report* I'd picked up from a street vendor on Melrose Avenue about how our economy is collapsing). I tried to settle in and wait for the drink cart. As people nested into their seats a couple came up the aisle with two small children. He—early 50s and on his second time around from my guess, and she—a youngish late 30s with collagen lips and silicon torpedoes. She was wearing a suede baseball cap. I figured they were on their way back to Aspen or the likes.

It wasn't long before the older of the two children started to scream. Making the other one scream. The two kids were kind of jammed between the two parents in a three-seater, the mother on my side just across the aisle. Having been so keenly aware since waking, of the passage of time and how to spend it making completely sure of getting out of this city—once on the plane I lost it. I no longer had to do anything but sit back. Nothing I could do but pass the time and let it happen. But I couldn't relax with all that screaming. I glanced over and watched as the Aspen Mom offered the screaming child first a sip from a super-sized Coca-Cola, then a Girl Scout sugar cookie from a small plastic baggie. That did it. I leaned over and in a voice that I have to admit was at a level designed to stretch a couple of rows at least I kindly suggested that between the sugar and caffeine in the drink, and the sugar and carbs in the cookies, physiologically her child might as well be smoking crack.

It is truly amazing how unreceptive some parents can be to helpful advice, graciously offered from the bottom of one's heart, on how they may better raise their children.

She turned around and gave me a shocked look, her bizarre poofed and brown lipsticked mouth parting in kind of a "how could you" expression that gave me encouragement. I had her attention so I spoke again. "At this rate you'll have him on Ritalin within five years, guaranteed." Feeling I had dropped the other shoe, I calmly went back to reading about the financial collapse in our future not noticing her hand calmly rising to hit the "Assistance" button above her.

"Ding"

At first I paid no mind to the female flight attendant whose butt was cheek to cheek with my face. But when the guy came down the aisle with the metal wings on his lapels and stern expression I instinctively looked up. It was at this point I realized we were still sitting at the gate. My mind flashed back to the annoying lady who had insisted her son bought her a first class seat, making such a ruckus that the plane returned to the terminal.

The official looking guy, who was either a steward, male flight attendant, or the co-pilot, approached and spread himself the width of the aisle putting his hands on the backs of the chairs in front of us both. "What seems to be the problem ma'am?" he asked, looking directly at me. "This man accosted me," she began. That actually amused me and I blurted out with an astonished smile, "Accosted? ACCOSTED?" Then a helpful voice in the back of my head said something like, "Shut up you fool...you're going to get thrown off."

"He said my baby was smoking crack and taking Ritalin!" At this all I could do was shake my head. Her two children screamed. The guy looks at me again and says, "I'll go talk with the captain." I was fucked. After all the bumbling and confusion I had managed to end up on my flight. And now, because of my big mouth, I'm going to get tossed. What a complete idiot.

After a couple of agonizing minutes, the man stormed back up the aisle. I sat frozen in fear. "The captain says you can either get off the plane or sit where I tell you." "I'll do anything you say," I answered as earnestly and humbly as I could. I was moved a few rows back, close to the rear toilet. I couldn't believe that I'd escaped expulsion.

I was seated next to a couple who had flown out of Hawaii. They shoveled fast food out of Styrofoam containers. We made no contact, eye or otherwise, the entire trip. I felt myself a criminal of conscience. The plane pulled away from the gate. It seemed like I didn't even breathe until the landing gear had retracted and I felt us climb.

Through all of this the husband said nothing nor did he attempt to make eye contact with me. He walked past me twice during the flight to bring each child, bladders bursting with Coke no doubt, to the rear restroom. He said nothing all four passes back and forth. I took him to be a coward. On re-telling this story to friends some suggest that perhaps he agreed with me. One can only hope so for the sake of the children's health. To my surprise and relief, I was allowed without question or warning to purchase a Heineken. I only ordered one because I didn't want to get out of line.

A few days after I got back to Boulder I received an email from The Palms Thai Restaurant:

```
"I saw ozzy osbourne at my restaurat on 3.22.03 at
7 o'clock he wanted me to take a picture with him
and i wanted to know whthis card is because ozzy
told me that i have to give this to my dad and i
think that he won't know whatg this card is? Thank
you, krischana."
```

Whit had taken a shot of the girl and me with my little disposable box camera. At the restaurant I handed the girl my business card, instructing her to give it to her dad (so he wouldn't think I was trying some weirdo Internet thing) and have him email me their street address so I could send a copy. Apparently The Thai Elvis isn't all that tech savvy for it was his daughter who sent the email. I put a print of the shot in an envelope and dropped it in a mailbox. No note, no fake autograph of course—just the shot of the two of us smiling. I wonder to this day if they've figured out I wasn't the real Ozzy. But I didn't want to ruin it for The Thai Elvis' daughter if she hadn't.

9

Sleeping with Sandra Bullock

"How the fuck is a legend supposed to feel?
Do they wake up in the morning and go,
'Oh darling, I feel very legend-ly this morning?'"
- Ozzy Osbourne

By the summer of 2003 the two women who were running competing look-alike conventions in Vegas were at each other's throats. With the two, almost identical-in-nature conventions scheduled less than a week apart, the look-alikes had to either suffer the economic hardship of making two trips to Las Vegas or staying for almost two weeks. At first I was going to choose the one featuring the most seminars that looked educational and interesting, then I got a call from Elyse.

"I've found your Sandra."

This changed my plans immediately. Even though it was largely in jest, I had put it out into the universe months earlier, in newspapers, video interviews and on the Web, that I was looking to sleep with a Sandra Bullock look-alike. Somehow Elyse had run across one and had convinced her to come to Vegas. Of course, she availed "Sandra" of all my previous PR mentioning my supposed amorous aims. It was a strange and exciting situation for me. Along with the "be careful what you wish for" aspect, maybe this would be more fun than I had counted on.

I was already booked for the competing convention, so I quickly made travel plans to cover the first couple of days of Elyse's as well. I just couldn't take the time off of work to do both. My buddy Austin Powers called me a few days after I'd made my arrangements. "Are you ready for this?" he tempted me, "I just did a radio show with a bunch of look-alikes and Elyse showed up with another Ozzy." This news hit me like a brick in the face. I guess I can't blame Elyse for working every angle, and having two Ozzys is certainly better than one (especially when I refused to sign an exclusive with her). But baiting me with the Sandra Bullock and not mentioning the other Ozzy pissed me off. I called and left a nasty message on her answering machine suggesting that somehow I'd been betrayed.

My problem with the whole "business" end of the look-alike madness is that I really didn't want to be bothered with a paid appearance, yet I hated yielding any ground to an interloper. It was a silly position to take, and I knew I was out of line, but my emotions and competitive spirit got the best of my common sense. Ultimately I ended up apologizing to Elyse and sending her flowers to celebrate her engagement to her new boyfriend Howard.

Austin wanted to meet me at the airport in a chauffeur's uniform and take me back to the hotel in his vintage Rolls Royce. He urged me to dress like Ozzy, meet him at baggage claim and we'd "make a scene" while his wife videotaped it. With the post- 9/11 security at airports stepped up, I had no desire whatsoever to make a scene anywhere in or near an airport, so I declined his kind offer. The heat in Vegas was punishing. Almost as soon as the sun came up the desert went to 90+ and it was too hot to leave the confines of the hotel. This suited me fine, though, as I mainly wanted to party this time around and meet the Sandra.

Elyse told me that Sandra was due in the next day and would be cabbing directly from the airport to the golf putting tournament that had been arranged for the look-alikes and the press. I couldn't wait. This was a fantasy coming true. Elyse had mentioned that a documentary crew from A&E would be covering the convention, but it turned out to air on AMC (American Movie Classics) as part of their *AMC Project:* series. *Project: Lookalike* was directed by up and coming, Sundance-winning documentary filmmaker Jonathan Karsh. A wiry fireball of positive energy, he reminded me a lot of Jenny Jones' producer Jim. I was on my way to the pool-side cocktail reception when the crew caught me.

I had my Sandra routine down pat by this time and it rolled off my tongue on camera like a practiced act. I had learned that if you pause, you die, so I tried to string it all together and this time it worked. It consisted of:

- Needed a good line for reporters in Vegas for the convention last year
- Came up with "I want to sleep with Sandra" concept on the fly at cocktail reception
- Ended up getting good visibility in four different newspapers because of the line
- Elyse found a Sandra and I will meet her for the first time tomorrow
- I am so excited and I didn't know what to expect

I got through it flawlessly if I do say so myself. Jonathan yelled, "Cut!" and the whole crew laughed. Karsh remarked, "That's great."

As someone who made documentary films in high school and college, I knew I had given them something they could build on if they chose to. I was trying to create some tension and make it funny, but was starting to feel some tension myself. What had I started? What would the fake Sandra expect from me? I had a choice between stressing out about it or enjoying myself. Finding my way to the area where they had the look-alikes grazing a lunch buffet, I joined them feeling relieved I'd done my bit for the camera. Now I could relax.

Karsh's crew crawled around the party and pool area while the various look-alikes aped for the gaping tourists, lying around like so many beached white whales. I would grab the really good Will Smith from England or Rodney Dangerfield and walk amongst the sunbathing bikinis, flirting shamelessly and making them giggle. Life was good.

I spent the first evening sitting around the casino bar at The Imperial Palace with Willie Nelson and Jack Nicholson waiting for Austin and his wife to join us, which they finally did rather late. Austin, his wife and I, took off to have dinner at The Bahama Breeze in full costume. Our dinner was punctuated by tourists asking for photographs. I talked excitedly about meeting Sandra, and stressed about what I had gotten myself into with my big mouth. Was she expecting something of me? Was I supposed to come on to her? Should I play it cool? What if she looks nothing like Sandra? Austin just shook his head sadly from side to side and said in his *actual* British accent, "Shag 'er, mate, what's the big deal?"

Sandra was to arrive the next day while all the look-alikes were going to be at the press event. There is an 18-hole putting course on the outskirts of town that was to be the first opportunity to meet the media while we played a round. Elyse is good at setting these kinds of things up.

All the look-alikes met in the hotel lobby around 9:30am to load into a bus for the golf course. I had a couple of breakfast beers in the room as I put on my Ozzy gear and brought another with me to the bus queue that caused only a few errant stares. Hey...it's Vegas and I'm Ozzy...my character would have been up all night!

Stepping onto the bus was Austin Powers, Anna Nicole Smith, two Kenny Rogers, Michael Jackson, Snoop Dog, John Cleese, Tina Turner, Kosmo Kramer Jack Nicholson, Sean Connery, two Whoopie Goldbergs, Willie Nelson, Carmen Miranda, Rodney Dangerfield, Neil Diamond, Tony Soprano, Keanu Reeves, and others. We looked like a magical mystery tour from Hollywood.

Not only was it beastly hot but Ozzy's outfit is all black. Planning ahead, I had purchased an umbrella at the gift shop. Later this would make me a very popular fellow. The first thing I looked for at the golf course was the bar. As it turned out, the place was so new that the liquor license hadn't cleared and it was to be a dry event—that put me in a fowl mood. Trapped miles from nowhere in the desert heat with no beer.

Making my mood a notch darker, the Other Ozzy showed up. That's all I need...competition. I guess it was only a matter of time. Great. Now I have to fight for face time. My reptile brain was telling me if he got anywhere near Sandra when she arrives I'd have to take him out somehow. He turned out to be a nice enough guy, an actual heavy metal guitar player. But like most heavy metal guitar players I've ever met, a tad brain dead. He couldn't do a British accent or care as far as I could tell and, as Johnny Carson reportedly remarked about Chevy Chase, "He couldn't improvise a fart after a baked bean meal." But his presence alone pissed me off. Consciously I liked to treat the whole look-alike thing as a joke, but subconsciously I guess it wasn't. If my hackles rise at the notion of competition, there must be some part of me taking it very seriously. A brief scene of the two Ozzys on the scorching putting green would find its way into the AMC documentary.

I like playing golf but my short game isn't all that good. Austin, who claimed he'd never played in his life, was sinking incredible putts. Snoop Dog complained loudly that, "This isn't the kind of green I'm used to," to any video crew he could find. A great line. I was hiding under my umbrella from the relentless sunrays but a stiff wind kept blowing it around. Sensing an opportunity for a bit, I tapped a cameraman on the shoulder and said, "Watch this." I let the wind blow the umbrella out of my hand, and then yelling "Sharon...SHARON!" I chased the umbrella around the course, kicking it away from me with expert comedic clumsiness each time I was upon it.

This went over well enough that I had to repeat it for three different camera crews. At least I had a routine that was working. But all of that running around in what was now 100 degrees was going to give me a heart attack. There were ice tubs full of plastic bottles of spring water placed around the course. I took to pouring them over my head to try to cool off (plus, Ozzy drenches himself in performance all the time, so it was in character). When Sandra finally appeared walking toward the course, in to me what seemed like slow motion, I was out of breath and panting and had the appearance of a drowned rat in round blue sunglasses.

I dropped my club, told the others in my foursome to carry on without me and walked up to meet her. She was wearing a light blue dress and a sash reading: "MISS CONGENIALITY." She looked enough like Sandra to me. I introduced myself, and tried to maintain a bit of cool, since I didn't know how all of this was going to turn out. I was too embarrassed to even mention all the comments I'd made to the press about sleeping with someone doing what she was doing. I knew she knew, so I just held back.

Sandra was already a model in New York, and had been told by enough people that she looked like Bullock to go for it. I started walking her around the course, introducing her to the other lookalikes and giving her advice on how to get some decent face time with the cameramen. One crew came up and asked if they could get some tape and they asked me to step aside after I'd done my bit so they could get Sandra solo. I was standing behind the camera operator when the interviewer asked Sandra, "So, are you married?" to which she replied, "Yes," and I let out an unintentional and very loud "D'oh!" causing them to have to do a re-take. She laughed. The cameraman didn't. I hadn't thought to ask her and hadn't checked her finger for a ring. This changed everything all of a sudden and now my mood was really at risk. I was performing without beer in the goddam desert, there were two Ozzys, Sandra is married and the day was still young. Oh well, I decided to try to make the best of it anyway.

She told the camera crew that she only had one Sandra routine. She did a short speech as Gracie Hart the FBI agent from *Miss Congeniality*, with an authentic, thick New Jersey accent that unfortunately turned out to be her normal speaking voice. "Not too Sandra-like," I thought to myself, slightly disappointed. "I can do The Nanny too," she offered, "Please don't," I thought silently.

One of my problems is that I can't maintain my cool around women. If I like them it's too obvious, as in "stop humping my leg." I promised myself I wouldn't make that mistake with Sandra, even if she was married and I wasn't going to be realizing any fantasies anytime soon. I just get carried away because it's fun.

I went back to goofing around the course and fending off other look-alikes' attempt to borrow my precious life-saving sun-masking umbrella. Carmen Miranda pleaded to borrow it, "Ah got eight pounds uh froot own mah hay-yed...can't ah git undah they-ya fo' uh lil' while?" Anna Nicole was a bit more direct, grabbing my ass and shouting, "Gimme that umbrella bitch!" We gathered for one last group shot and the outing was over.

It came time to leave and to my delight Sandra walked up to me and asked if I'd help her with her bags. She had come to the course directly from the airport and had several large pieces. We dragged them to the shuttle bus while I made nervous small talk. I told her that my favorite Sandra quote was the "You think I'm gorgeous...you want to kiss me...you want to date me..." song from *Miss Congeniality*. Sandra started singing it as we threw her bags into the bus and she had me. (And now she had two routines.)

On the bus back to the hotel I continued to dispense advice on the business of look-alikes. I sat in the seat across the aisle so as not to crowd her. As we got to The Imperial Palace I suggested she insist on a non-smoking room because they would probably claim they didn't have any available. She asked, "What floor are you on?" and I told her the 10th. She proceeded to step over the velvet ropes and cut to the front of the line. "You can't do that," I protested, "I'm from New Yawk," she answered over her shoulder.

My floor was booked and she ended up on the floor above. I helped her get her bags into the elevator, got as far as my floor, asked if she was okay to get the rest of the way herself and she said she was. "Want to meet in a little while for lunch? I'm starving," she said. "Sure!" We agreed to meet downstairs in twenty minutes.

Sandra and I found a restaurant inside the hotel that appealed to her. I wasn't hungry (too nervous) so I just had a beer while she had a sandwich. I continued with my mini-seminar on the look-alike business, trying to recount for her all that I'd learned and as many recollections that I could dredge up about my experiences. Because of slow service we were there for about an hour. During lunch I told her what De Niro Joe Manuella had taught me about having promotional material with you at all times, having a set routine ready to go, listening to your character in your car as you drive around, etc. She attacked the sandwich and listened intently. Sandra asked how much money was to be made in this business and I mentally totaled up all of the requests and leads the agents had fed me over the last year. "I'd say on the high side maybe five or six grand, and Ozzy's hot right now." At this, a piece of sandwich lodged in Sandra's throat and she began to cough violently. Trying to make light of it I said, "If I have to apply the Heimlich maneuver can I hand my camera to a tourist first? That would make a great shot." Her laughter brought her breathing back. We were only a couple of hours away from the big barbecue event at producer John Stuart's ranch, so we both went back to our rooms to get ready.

It was 3:10pm by this time and my room still hadn't been made up. I called Housekeeping, "Hello, I'm in room 1016 and would like my room made up." An unintelligible Asian woman answered, "Whotta yoo say?" "I said I'm in room 1016 and would like it made up please." "Teen sex fiend?" the Asian woman asked. "NO! room one, zero, one, six." Within a couple of minutes an Asian woman appeared with a supply cart and vacuum. "No can do loom with you here – me come back rater." We negotiated a ten-minute window in which she could straighten things up. "Jus' pirrow cases then...no bed." "Yes, fine, I'll be back in ten minutes, thank you very much." I went down to the canteen to buy some more Buds.

At the little shop on the lobby level another Asian lady checked me out as she took my money for the beers. "Ozzy hail dahkah...'n' yoo too tarr," she offered. Too tall and my hair isn't dark enough. Thanks. I'll make a note of that.

Back at my room, with a fresh tub of cold Buds, I was tired of wearing the Ozzy crap. I didn't think the Barbecue event was going to be open to the press (and I wanted Sandra to see the "real me") so I dressed in civilian clothes for the occasion, which turned out to be a huge mistake. By the time I met up with the rest of the talent I had gone through half of my Bud stash—both kinds. In short, I was bombed and dressed in civvies looking like just another drunken tourist.

Queuing up for the bus to the ranch, I noticed Sandra was nowhere to be seen and began to get nervous. Did I miss her? Is there more than one bus? I ran to the big bus at the head of the line of three and found her and one empty seat close by. She was dressed casually as well, in a kind of hiking outfit, tan shorts and a tee shirt. This time she'd chosen her "Short Sandra" wig. At this point I realized the long hair I saw on the golf course wasn't hers, which was kind of a shock. She was dressed as the *Speed* Sandra.

Sitting next to her on the bus is what we in the look-alike business refer to with pity as "a Delusional." This is a person who has, no doubt, had friends tell him that he looks like Keanu Reeves, but he doesn't. I'm sorry. People had to ask him who he "was." He had locked onto Sandra pretty tightly. Tony Soprano, sitting one row behind her was beginning to make his move. With the cunning of a Las Vegas drunk, I hung back and watched the two guys destroy themselves with her.

We were still parked waiting for the others to load up and I yelled out, "Let Sandra drive the bus!" "What?" a few of the look-alikes asked. "Yeah, like in *Speed*." The bus driver smiled and stepped aside. I took a couple of shots of her posing like she was driving the bus with my camera and with hers.

Even though it was going on sunset, the heat was still punishing as we rumbled off on our way to John Stuart's ranch—the ranch that look-alikes built. It's a beautiful place with lots of horses and lots of land. The entire back of the house had been decked out for the party with a huge catered chow line, a gazebo the size of a small house and a performing trio of cowboy singers under a green awning off the back.

I was too nervous to be as hungry as I should have been. I was also thrown off by the number of press people at the event—and here I am in my regular clothes. I was as anti-Ozzy as I could get: bright yellow Polo shirt, light gray slacks, brown suede shoes. In short, a fat middle-age dork. Oh well. I tried like hell to leave Sandra alone, still not wanting to crowd her. Tony Soprano was shadowing her every move. I watched from a distance. He's an extra large Tony Soprano, so I didn't feel like my manhood was being threatened. Plus they're both Italians so I assumed they were bonding on that level as well.

I invited the Other Ozzy to join me behind the horse barn for a quick toke. He spoke of selling an amp to Keith Richards once, and I told him my story of having to wrest my own 1959 Fender Bassman amp from British rocker Dave Edmunds at a repair shop in Los Angeles, and selling vintage Vox amps to Jackson Browne in the 80s. One of the Vox AC-30s I traded Browne for some AV gear he no longer needed even got a *credit* on Bonnie Raitt's *Luck of the Draw* album: "...and an extra special thanks to Jackson Browne for his hellacious Vox Amp." This haunts me to this day—the damned amp is more famous than I am.

The two Ozzys now pleasantly buzzed, walked back to the open bar. I was getting another cold one when someone tapped my shoulder, "The guy playing is asking where Ozzy is." He pointed me at the trio on the back porch. I carefully made my way (weaved is more like it) up to the stage and went on Remote Control. I joined the guitarist/singer and grabbed the gut bucket (a single stringed "instrument" comprised of a wash tub, a broom handle and a string of taut animal gut) to play bass accompaniment on Hank Williams' *Kaw Liga*. The song choice made especially appropriate as I was standing next to an actual wooden Indian, the subject of the song. We sounded pretty good and looking up during the performance I was delighted to see Sandra had moved toward the front and was taking photos of me. After completing the number to warm applause I noticed the camera lights go on in the huge gazebo. I pointed this out to Sandra and said, "Let's go get some face time."

We found a place to sit on the gazebo's steps and waited for the crew to finish their interview with Tony Soprano. They composed a two shot, Sandra and some dork in a yellow shirt. I took my hair out of the ponytail so I would at least look a bit like Ozzy as tape rolled. I listened to Sandra's story about how enough people insisted she looked like the character for her to act on it. Then I interjected, "Hey, can I ask her a question?" The director said sure. I asked, "How is it that your husband allowed you to fly thousands of miles to meet a guy who is on record saying he wants to sleep with you?" I surprised myself. It just came out. But I was actually curious by this time.

She looked directly into the camera lens and said, "My husband is a construction worker—he can't even turn on my computer much less read my email." This shocked me and I turned to the camera saying, "When he sees this interview I'm a dead man." This put things in a different perspective, but I wasn't exactly sure how to evaluate it. Soon after this we noticed that the busses were loading up for trips back to the hotel every fifteen minutes. We hopped the first one.

Back at the hotel, the plan was to get into our characters' clothes, meet up and go to the Frontier. "I haven't checked my email in a day and a half...do you have a computer?" she asked. I offered to let her use my laptop and she followed me to my room. I was happy that the maid had finally straightened the place up, and nervously paced while this woman sat on my bed tapping away on my keyboard. I'm easily flustered. She finished up quickly and we agreed on a time to meet. "I'll come by your room and pick you up," she suggested.

My buddy Austin Powers runs a karaoke show every Sunday night at The Frontier Hotel and had encouraged any and all look-alikes to drop by and sing a number that evening. I was prepared in advance for this, Sandra or no, and was going to do a rendition of *Mama I'm Coming Home*. I'd bought the karaoke version of the song for this purpose and after working with Austin to ramp the song's pitch down a couple of keys (something his karaoke setup can do digitally without affecting the song's tempo) I was confident I could deliver a good performance.

When Sandra came by the room she was in her *Miss Congeniality* outfit again and had the "Long Sandra" wig on. It was like a dream date in a way, and I was definitely approaching a dream state due to the heat, the exhaustion, the beer and the pot. We proceeded downstairs, in full regalia, through the lobby, waving and causing a minor ruckus.

Outside it was still hot, even this late at night, and I was wearing the ankle-length reverend's coat and immediately began to sweat. It was obvious from the long line of tourists that it was going to take some time to get a cab. Measuring up the situation here we stood, both in costume, in a long line of plain people. I couldn't take it. We not only did not feel very special standing there, but we both might as well have been dressed for Halloween. The situation was poised to become embarrassing. I asked the doorman, "Is there any better way to get a cab?" He motioned at a stretch limo, "Forty bucks and just tell him where to go—no waiting." This appealed to me so I went for it. It turned out to be one of the better decisions I'd made in an otherwise stressful day.

The limo was cool, air-conditioned cool too, ringed with tiny lights inside, long, quiet, and cushy. It was a true escape from the outside world, and as we slowly cruised down the strip I allowed myself to deeply enjoy the moment. Here I was with Sandra Bullock on my way to a Las Vegas stage performance. How many photos of celebrities getting out of limos had I studied in *16 Magazine* and *Datebook*, *Tiger Beat* and the rest. Even though the entire scenario was fake, it felt real enough to seriously dig.

Arriving at the Frontier, we caused the usual commotion walking in. We negotiated our way through the drunks in the showroom yelling "Ozzy!" wanting photographs. We approached the stage (now Gilleys) where, I'm told, Elvis made his first Las Vegas appearance. Austin gestured me over and we discussed when I was to go on. On one side was a mechanical bull where tourists were lined up to have a 20 second spine-injuring thrill ride—most falling to the floor in the first five. The guy at the controls had a big tip jar next to him. The game was, when your buddy gets on the bull, you slip the fellow at the controls a ten and say "Hurt him."

Austin signaled that it was my turn on stage. He cued up "Mama" and I yelled to the crowd "Show me your lighters!" (Ozzy's signal to his concert audience he's about to sing a ballad). To my delight the crowd screamed and lighters were held high all over the room. I started weaving back and forth, waving my arms high above my head during the instrumental introduction. I had a devious plan. Instead of singing, "Mama I'm coming home..." I was going to look directly at her and sing, "Sandra, I'm coming home" instead. The crowd moved closer to the stage. I saw her taking pictures. This was going great.

The song ended and the crowd reaction was strong enough that Austin insisted I stay on stage for an encore—with him!

Austin wanted to sing Ozzy's *Paranoid* and have me support him onstage. There wasn't a part for me to sing so I just ran around and acted crazy, causing the karaoke machine to skip repeatedly. "Would you stop leaping about?" he pleaded during one such interruption. The crowd laughed. When I jumped off stage Sandra walked up and said, "Let's go to the Hard Rock Cafe."

We walked through the Hard Rock to the usual tourist reaction. We tried to get into the VIP room but were turned away. It was late so we decided to head back to the hotel. When we hit the Imperial it was past 2am. Sandra said, "Come up to my room...I'd like to give you some pictures." As soon as I entered her room I became very uncomfortable. Here I was in a married woman's room, in Las Vegas, in the middle of the night. While she rummaged through her belongings, pulling out head shots and modeling composites, I suddenly felt like a trapped animal, although I wasn't. I was the one in the fantasy world—she was professionally indifferent, but I was freaking nonetheless.

All of the hard work throughout the two days, giving her space, not crowding, hanging back, etc., had resulted in enough trust, or so it seemed, that she felt comfortable inviting me into her private quarters. But at this point, I could easily blow it and knew it. Sandra laid the photos out side by side on the dresser. Looking at the shots I noticed that none of them, though obviously professionally taken, showed an open-mouth smile. "Why no teeth in any of these?" I asked. "You have a pretty smile." With that she melted a little as I moved for the door, realizing I had just inadvertently complimented her looks, which could have been interpreted as a pass, or so I thought at the moment. She followed too closely and I turned to say goodnight. It was obvious a hug was in order, so after that, backing into the hotel hallway I shook her hand, told her I'd had a wonderful time and so long until next time (I was on a plane home in the morning).

On the flight home I began to think about fantasy versus reality. The Ozzy thing is based on reality, so that's easy enough to compartmentalize. The fake Ozzy wanting to have carnal relations with a fake Sandra is easy to comprehend too, I guess. But having to deal with that possibility in the flesh was not something I suspected I was going to have to do. Would I have "gone through with it" had she been single and willing? Would I have asked her to leave her wig on? Would she want me to stay made up as Ozzy? It was all too bizarre to process. I was content to feel like one of my fantasies had been realized. Kind of, anyway, and I'd apparently made a new friend. Months later I would help her put a website together and instruct her on how to get into a look-alike Web ring (series of sites of similar or same subject matter).

Just a week later I was on a plane back out to Las Vegas to attend the second look-alike convention. The previous year the International Guild of Celebrity Impersonators and Tribute Artists (IGCITA) and Elyse cooperated on one convention, but due to the rivalry, this year there was competition for attendees at two different events just days apart. The situation with the two conventions was as contentious as it was unnecessary, but neither one of the organizers was going to give an inch.

Elyse is more media focused, but the other convention had some interesting presentations I wanted to see. One in particular was a local Fox broadcaster Dale Russell's "The Devil in My Doorway" talk about how to handle being interviewed by a potentially hostile reporter. His advice was casually delivered and good.

Forget about the concept of a monolithic media; you will usually be dealing one-on-one with a single individual, and every reporter is different. Read the reporter's bio. A media reporter can be a tremendous advantage or do tremendous damage. An encounter with the media is a business transaction so treat it as one.

Understand the difference between media and what you can expect. With radio you might get 30 seconds and a single good quote. With a newspaper story you have more of a chance for some depth. Television might allow two quotes, but feeds on visuals, so be prepared for the camera. Remember that radio and television in any market feed off the press.

Present yourself to the media before you'll need it. Be a friend of the press. The press loves availability, so be easy to reach. Journalists are on deadline and have to work fast. Have your materials on file with major media outlets in advance. A reporter would much rather deal directly with you (the talent) than an agent or PR person.

Know your message, be ready to stress the most important point you're trying to get across (e.g., "I would like to sleep with someone who looks like Sandra Bullock,"). A good reporter is interested in the truth, and will try to knock you off your message. What's your hook? Is your character's birthday coming up? Is he appearing in town?

It was a good session filled with good advice. Wrapping up a day's worth of workshops was Richard Skipper, a Carol Channing impersonator. Mr. Skipper was adamant that he is not an impersonator, he is a *tribute artist*. I have no great love for Carol Channing the entertainer. In fact seeing her occasionally on television growing up I found her annoying. But this Skipper guy loves her with such a passion, and he has dedicated himself to becoming her on stage, that I couldn't help but get drawn into his trip. His description of actually meeting Channing for the first time brought tears to my eyes.

Later that evening the convention goers were to be treated to an evening of entertainment featuring Will Collins as Liberace – at Liberace's own theater! I prepared by drinking Buds and getting my Ozzy crap on. I didn't want to chance that this was going to be a press event like the John Stuart ranch meal when I dressed as a dork.

"I hate everything there is to hate about England"
- The Angry Elvis

We all piled into a few shuttle busses for the trip to Liberace's. There was an Italian restaurant in the front that adjoined the little theater. We sat on long benches, ate, drank, yelled, laughed and screamed. Thankfully it was a closed party. I sat with Johnny Cash and a fellow I came to know as The Angry Elvis. The Angry Elvis was in from England. Although an American, he had lived in London for many years and hated it. Hated the food, hated the people, hated the country, but that's where he lived. He sat there looking just like Elvis, bitching about England. Johnny Cash looked to be about 70 years old, with a jet black toupee. He was a riot, and we haunted the bar for most of the evening waiting for the show to begin, telling each other rude jokes.

Eventually the door opened and we piled into the little theater. I got a comfortable seat and settled in for what was one of the more gay shows I'd seen in awhile. They had made an effort to incorporate some of the look-alikes from the convention and Michael Jackson and Will Smith did great "star" turns during a rousing dance number. A sub-standard Rodney Dangerfield did knee-slapping Dangerfield material, and of course, Liberace and Carol Channing minced all over the place.

I didn't bother to go to any of the workshops the second day of the convention. I knew what to expect. I slept late and wandered down to the ballroom to pick at what was left over from the lunch buffet. I ran into Johnny Cash, as bored as I was, and we decided that we might as well go see some tits before that evening's gala awards ceremony. We cabbed over to the Flamingo to catch what is billed as the longest running afternoon show in Vegas. Breck Wall's *Bottom's Up!* has been going, two shows a day, for over 40 years. *Bottom's Up!* is old fashioned vaudeville filled with bad and bawdy jokes, a few dance numbers and some breasts. It was a good excuse to relax for a while, have a couple of laughs, get to know another look-alike and have a couple of beers while admiring some titties. Standing in line in our outfits, Johnny and Ozzy didn't draw too many tourists but received special attention from the little old lady at the door of the theater. "I guess you boys would like to sit right down front huh?" she said, as she thrust her upturned palm into my leg. I was a little tipsy so I didn't get the hint right away. "Right" —*poke*—"up" —*poke*—"front" —*poke*. "Oh!" I finally got it and fished around for a bill to hand her. All I had was a five, but it got us the front row.

Johnny Cash and I got back to the hotel with plenty of time to pre-pare for the awards ceremony and entertainment showcase. The showcases are sometimes painful, as everyone gets a chance, whether they're talented or not, to do five minutes and the evening's fight card was getting quite long. My buddy Austin Powers had agreed to supply the sound system for the evening in return for a free pass to the con-vention and prime positioning in the showcase. We passed him in the hall as he loaded some speaker enclosures into the ballroom. He said there were too many performers and that the night was going to last forever.

The evening started with Austin doing his *Split Personality* song fol-lowed by a slew of look-alikes, some talented, some not. Angry Elvis had a very bad time of it. He couldn't get his mic to work right and then his Elvis belt came un-done. He broke every show business rule by stopping right there and saying, "Aww...to hell with it," and stomped off stage. During the nearly three-hour show I made repeated visits to the room to take smoke breaks.

On the way out of town, going through security, I was pulled aside by a TSA officer. "What have I done now?" I wondered. Even though I was in my civilian clothes, my hair pulled back and clear glasses on, the question was familiar: "Has anyone ever told you that you look like..." I handed him an Ozzy card and smiled my way to the gate.

By November of 2003 I had forgotten about the convention and the camera crews when I got the voicemail from Jonathan Karsh. "Call me right away please, we're wrapping up the editing and I'd like to talk with you." When I reached him he had one question: "So, uh, did you and Sandra, like, hook up?" Because I work with young people in their 20s I knew this meant, "Did you two have sexual relations thus fulfilling your fantasy and if so would you please tell me about it?" "Speaking as a gentleman," I began, "No, of course not. But seeing as how I am not a gentleman I'll tell you the truth. I have to admit, sadly no—I didn't sleep with Sandra." A month and a half later, the program was aired.

"AMC is running the show!" an instant message from Sandra popped up on my desk in mid January of 2004. "Monday night at 8pm EST!" It had been some time since an "Ozzy Incident" and my excitement and anticipation grew. I checked the AMC site and their review mentioned Robert De Niro and Nicole Kidman (who was not at the convention). At first the fact that it didn't mention me was a concern, but then I put American Movie Classics together with the look-alike convention and realized most of the look-alikes are of movie characters and this really wasn't my arena. I calmed down.

The show, *AMC Project: Lookalike* was a close look at three look-alikes within the context of the convention where a lot of other impersonators got their individual scenes. I appear in a couple of shots, one standing next to the Other Ozzy while the narrator says, "Think you're seeing double?" Featured was Joe Manuella, the fantastic Robert De Niro. He got about fifteen of the twenty-eight minutes it seemed, and I was delighted for him. Joe had been so supportive, kind and helpful to me from the first day I met him. The show mentioned his brush with the law and the fact he didn't want to discuss it. I can only tell you that Joe is a wonderful guy who must have at some point gotten carried away. Something only a few people (look-alikes) will probably ever truly understand.

I felt a sense of pride mixed with jealousy when they spent quite a bit of time on Sandra. She was the newcomer and the way they edited it reinforced the doubts she expressed as asides. They clearly had an angle on her, but she was getting face time so who cared? It's all about face time. Before one commercial break they showed me on the putting green, and due to my new technique of looking at the hole instead of the ball while putting, there were seconds more of my face than would have otherwise been the case. I called the parents who were watching at the same time in Louisville, Kentucky. "I'm happy with that. If that's all I get I can live with it."

At the end of the half hour there was one of those typical montage sequences wrapping up what had happened to all of the characters since the filming. A brief scene of the look-alike was shown, followed by a title card.

> Scene: Rodney Dangerfield on stage. Title: *'Rodney Dangerfield' won the award for best impersonation of a comedian.*

> Scene: Robert De Niro working the crowd at a party. Title: *Joe Manuella continues to work as a Robert De Niro lookalike.* Another scene of Manuella. Title: *'De Niro' is on his third Joe Pesci.*

> Scene: Nicole Kidman typing at her computer. Title: *'Nicole Kidman' has started her own lookalike agency.*

> Scene: Snoop Dogg working the crowd outside a hotel. Title: *'Snoop Dogg' works as a real estate agent in Las Vegas.*

> Scene: President George W. Bush working the crowd inside a hotel. Title: *'George Bush' has worked non-stop since the election. He hopes George Bush is re-elected.*

Scene: Sandra Bullock reaches over and hugs Ozzy (me) on the golf course. Title: *'Sandra Bullock' has quit the lookalike business.*

WHAT!? I was stunned. Oh my god. Had my weirdness or anything I had said to Karsh caused Sandra to quit the business? Why did she have me build her a website that was shown in the documentary? I emailed her, "YOU'VE QUIT?" She responded a day later that she had not, that she burst into tears when she saw it on teevee and didn't have the slightest idea where Karsh got that idea.

I immediately felt I knew what had happened. In Karsh's "wrap up" of the editing, he was deciding which bits made the best stories. When Karsh called her, as he had me, and asked Sandra if we had become intimate in Vegas she freaked. I bet myself that she went so overboard on the phone with him, insisting he take any reference to that out, that Karsh "heard" that she was quitting the business. An honest and unfortunate mistake.

When Sandra contacted Jonathan via email he confirmed as much. He understood from their conversation that she had quit the lookalike business and had gone back to modeling. I suggested to her that "Usually any publicity is good publicity, but they declared you out of business and unless you make an issue of it, that's not good publicity. My god, this guy has told the world there's no use in calling you!" Any business the show would have brought her was now gone. I felt she had a good chance for a quick settlement if she threatened to sue. Surely production companies have insurance policies, (and if he was as smart as he was talented Karsh was recording those phone conversations, mine included). I told Sandra to ask Joe Manuella his advice on how to find a good lawyer. She did.

For me anyway, this episode taught me that a fantasy is a wish that you really don't want to come true. My fantasy of sleeping with Sandra Bullock took on a life of its own in ways I could have never invented or predicted. In the end it wasn't me who fucked Sandra; ironically, inadvertently and indirectly, it was Jonathan Karsh.

10

The Kentucky Derby

"I always cry when me and my wife go and see slurpy movies. I'm there in the cinema with red eyes and tears rolling down my cheeks, and the kids are coming up and saying, Hey Ozzy, Satan rules!"
- Ozzy Osbourne

The 2002 Kentucky Derby played a large part in my decision to have a few Ozzy pictures taken. Since then I'd had a wild year. The 2003 Churchill Downs client repeatedly asked, (I politely declined the first two requests), that I bring my Ozzy gear and at some point mess with the crowd and possibly even venture into the infield. Having grown up in Louisville and attending many Derbys as an outfield partier, the notion was interesting but potentially suicidal. Former Louisvillian Dr. Hunter S. Thompson wrote of the Churchill Downs' infield in his 1970 magazine piece: *The Kentucky Derby is Decadent and Depraved* thusly:

> The Derby, the actual race, was scheduled for late afternoon, and as the magic hour approached I suggested to Steadman that we should probably spend some time in the infield, that boiling sea of people across the track from the clubhouse. He seemed a little nervous about it, but since none of the awful things I'd warned him about had happened so far—no race riots, firestorms or savage drunken attacks—he shrugged and said, "Right, let's do it."
>
> To get there we had to pass through many gates, each one a step down in status, then through a tunnel under the track. Emerging from the tunnel was such a culture shock that it took us a while to adjust. "God almighty!" Steadman

muttered. "This is a . . . Jesus!" He plunged ahead with his tiny camera, stepping over bodies, and I followed, trying to take notes.

My assignment for Derby 2003 was to haunt Millionaire's Row for the Friday before Derby Day (The Oaks) and the following Saturday (The Kentucky Derby—The Run for the Roses) in search of celebrities to videotape. I arranged with Texas Web/Flash designer Trevor Dodd and Churchill Downs Web guy Jeremy to meet at the track the preceding Thursday for a run-through and some tests.

This meant flying out from Denver International on Wednesday evening. My flight landed in Chicago at about 10:30pm. The weather was bad, as was my feeling about what could happen. Looking at the flight arrival and departure monitors, our short hop into Louisville had been cancelled due to weather. Well that's a pisser. I found the United "help desk" and a line estimated to be about 90 minutes long by a helpful United don't-go-postal-person walking the velvet rope. This was the line wherein you might, you may, get a clue as to another airline's connecting flight.

I was drunk. So sue me. I had a few on the flight. I thought all I was going to have to do was get on this puddle jumper, hop in a cab when I got to Louisville and catch a good night's sleep. This was not to be so, and bad was turning to worse.

An olive-skinned young lady arrived at the back of this line of United refugees and after a few moments declared, "Fuck this," as she turned marching off toward the main terminal. "Hey, are you going to Louisville?" I asked, "Yeah," she replied over her shoulder, "and I'm going to get my bag. This is bullshit."

She was right. This was a clusterfuck and it was going on eleven pm. Really bad boogie. Flashing back to the situation at DIA in the blizzard, I had no desire to sleep strung between two payphones in a Red Cross blanket sling. I followed the young lady's angry sashay that in this stressful moment was, I have to admit, rather pleasant.

Arriving at the baggage carousels, we both approached the only person there in uniform who looked like he might have a clue. He did. We walked with him to a computer terminal where he entered our information and informed us that, "Your bags are on their way to Louisville on another flight." "Why can't *we* be on that flight?" the girl and I asked in unison. He gave us a tired look.

By this time, we'd been joined by a small crowd of others, obviously going south to Louisville, based on the number of large hat boxes the ladies were carrying (large and elaborate Derby hats are a tradition and women go all out.) A couple much drunker than I was decided to cab it to a nearby hotel and make a party of the evening. I thought about doing the same for a second, but needed to get to Louisville so I could be at the Downs the next day at noon, and I was beginning to panic. It was eleven thirty pm.

"We're fucked, " I said. "Let's rent a car," the olive-skinned girl suggested. "If you drive, I'll pay for it," I answered. I've been hammering beers since Denver...I can't see straight but I can rent a car no problem." Hearing this, and seeing us walking toward the rental car counters, two other women, who I thought knew each other but didn't, followed us. "You going to the Derby?" "Yeah, follow us." I figured the more potential drivers the more chance I'd arrive alive.

The Hertz desk shut down as we approached. Another bad sign. Enterprise had a guy behind the counter with a huge shit-eating grin. The girls, now three of them, hung back and chattered amongst themselves. I wobbled up to the desk and slurred as little as I could, "We'd like a small sedan to Louisville please." "One way?" he grinned. "Yes." He tapped at his keyboard. "I can do something for $350.00." "Whatever, let's do that." Handing him my credit card and driver's license he tapped some more. "Will you be the only driver sir?" "No, these ladies," gesturing behind me to the tight group of three concerned faces, "will be helping me out." The Enterprise guy looked at the girls and asked, "May I see some ID?"

This is when it really started to suck big time. The olive-skinned girl presented her card. "I can't take debit cards," The Enterprise man said. "That's all I have," she said. "Me too," the other girls said in turn. "What...what is it...a kind of self-control thing?" I hollered, getting a little panicky. They all nodded like it was something so obvious that mentioning it at all just screamed cluelessness.

"Fine. I'll drive." I said. At this point I was angry enough that the adrenalin took over and I was sobering up with a vengeance. As we dragged our bags, me with three strange chicks in tow, toward the Enterprise shuttle bus area I hissed, "As soon as we're beyond the parking lot, one of you is taking over!" It was going on midnight when we, the only people in the shuttle bus, were deposited across from a sad gray sedan with one hubcap missing. I kid you not. "We're not getting in that," I said to the shuttle driver as the skinny blonde girl started to cry. The driver got on his radio, then pointed across the aisle to a red somethingorother. "I can upgrade you to that." "Fine, we'll take it." I was losing it. I just wanted to get past the gates and go to sleep as someone else drove me to Kentucky.

I don't know exactly why or how I kicked into some kind of controlling gear that would cause me to say, "Just a little farther up the road here...I'm okay." I'm sure it was irresponsible, but I got a second wind and hadn't had a beer for four hours at this point so my rage propelled me southward toward Louisville—with three women trapped in close quarters, listening to me talk about myself. I was going to enjoy this. I didn't care if they did or not; I'd paid for the goddam car and now they're going to listen to my Ozzy story.

It wasn't ten minutes outside of the airport parking lot when the skinny blonde let out a pitiful, "I'm hungry, I haven't eaten all day." I groaned. The thought caught on like wildfire. "Me too." "Hey, there's a McDonalds up ahead." I had to regain control, of both the situation and my temper. "Let's get a little farther down the road until we stop for food okay? We've got a long drive ahead of us." No one offered to take the wheel.

Not being someone who enjoys short drives much less long ones, this trip would have been hell on a sunny day. The storm that grounded the planes? Turns out that wasn't jive. About forty-five minutes outside of Chicago we headed into a squall that made driving a visual guessing game. "Am I in my lane? What's that ahead?" It sucked. We were all so terrified that we talked a lot. Well, at least I talked a lot. The skinny blonde was going to visit a friend who was attending the University of Louisville. She'd been told that Derby was one big party. "Welcome to the party," I said, my eyes locked on what I hoped was the middle line.

The olive-skinned chick in the back seat was constantly on her cell phone speaking to the people in Louisville she was supposed to have met at the airport by now. This would continue through the night, even though in Louisville's EST time zone, it was now approaching dawn. The third was an artist, who lived on a farm and kept dogs. She sat up front. She was a singer in a band and they'd played a few gigs but their lives just got too busy to take it professionally. We talked about being single. I liked it. She didn't. "Do you like dogs?" she asked at one point. Silent miles followed.

The storm broke apart and let up about two and a half hours in. I begrudgingly turned into a Denny's somewhere between Chicago and Louisville. All the girls ran for the bathroom. I sat out front in the waiting area wondering how long all of this was going to take. Somebody got a coffee to go but I honestly don't remember any food being brought into the car. I was starting to operate on an unpleasant mixture of terror and exhaustion. All I had agreed to do was to take all of the girls to a central location in downtown Louisville, like a major hotel or a bus station, where they could get cabs. I wasn't asking them for any money for the ride, and hadn't asked anyone to take the wheel yet. But it was going to be four in the morning by the time we made Louisville and public transportation would be iffy at best. I had miles to kick myself around in an internal monologue, "What the hell is wrong with you, you take these women to wherever they need to go and shut up about it."

I resigned myself to my fate. I asked each girl where she wanted to be dropped off. The olive-skinned cell phone girl (each time she called Louisville the party in the hotel room was getting wilder): The Executive Inn at the airport. The skinny blonde: an upscale apartment complex close to U of L. The artist, thankfully out in St. Matthews, just a couple of miles from my parents' house where I was staying. Don's SuperShuttle!

"Jesus...this is going to take another 45 minutes," I thought to myself. But maybe there would be some karma points in it or something. As Bob De Niro said, "You never know who you're dealing with." The olive-skinned girl still had her cell phone to her ear when we pulled up in front of The Executive Inn. She waved goodbye, we hugged, and I was later to discover this is when I lost my prescription sunglasses. (I hate United.) I took the skinny blonde to her friend's, who was nice enough to come meet her outside at what was now 4:15am. On to St. Matthews with the remaining artist, then to bed. My parents were at a church function in Indiana and not home that evening. They were to return sometime in the morning so I put a note on the door that read, "Arrived at 5am – Please Do Not Disturb – Need Sleep."

I set the alarm for 11am and collapsed onto the guest bed. My plan was to get up, proceed to the Downs, do my tests, then come home and crash. The alarm clock went off before my parents made it back so around noon I headed out for the Downs with my Canon GL-1 and brand new Azden shotgun microphone. At Derby 2002 there was so much crowd noise that the celebrities were hard to hear—I hoped that a decent shotgun mic (uni-directional) in their face would help solve that. There were a couple of settings and I wanted to check both out.

I walked around the Downs interviewing a few of the Thursday patrons and brought the footage back to the "command center" in the Churchill Downs executive office suite (a cubicle that had been set aside for us). Trevor and I found settings that worked. My next stop was Louisville's Standiford Field to find my lost luggage. It still hadn't been located. Disgusted, unkempt, unshaven and unbelievably tired, I went home to try to rest up for the next day. By then the parents were back. I put on pajamas and let my 79 year-old mom bring me a snack. I went to bed early, slept the sleep of the dead and awoke ready for The Oaks.

I was able to grab a few interviews the first day: Sigourney Weaver, Secretary of Labor Elaine Chao, actor Matthew St. Patrick and Joe Millionaire among others. I ran around like a maniac. It was hot, but fun. Trevor, Jeremy, Randall and the Applied Trust Internet security guys were doing yeomen's work back at Command Central processing the video and uploading the compressed files. That night we had a team-building dinner at a downtown restaurant and instead of following my hometown instinct of partying with the Derby revelers, I wisely decided to go to bed early again.

Waking up on Derby Day in my hometown of Louisville, Kentucky is a special and nostalgic experience for me. Growing up, even a kid could feel the whole town rev up and put on the dog. Once a year Louisville had the entire world's attention for a few short minutes. The Kentucky Derby, more than tobacco, football, bourbon or basketball puts Louisville on the map once a year. It's an exciting day. When the weather is nice, it's Louisville decked out in her springtime best and Derby Day 2003 was such a day. I was driving to Churchill Downs, which is located in an otherwise seedy part of old Louisville, when heading down Eastern Parkway (near the neighborhood Dr. Hunter S. Thompson grew up in) I realized I was following a car with a vanity plate reading: "KY DERBY." I took this to be a good omen. Maybe I'd bet a few bucks

I reached an intersection several blocks away from the Downs where traffic was stopped by National Guardsmen. Within seconds I heard a chorus of sirens like I'd never heard before. What seemed to be a mile-long parade of police cars, marked and unmarked, but each with lights and sirens going began to snake toward the Downs at top speed. One cop after another. I saw one lone limousine in the middle of the caravan. Whoever the hell it was, they were important! I found a parking space (which is a trick, and a trek) a reasonable distance away from the Downs and paid the folks guarding the lot behind an abandoned factory. They'll make a few thousand dollars over the course of Derby weekend selling spaces at twenty bucks a pop. The locals lining Central Avenue and the surrounding streets do the same, letting cars pull right up on their lawns, selling spaces in front of their houses, running up and down the streets with signs saying "Last Chance to Park Before Downs." Barbeques burn on front porches all day as the locals watch the madness pass back and forth before them.

I had my video gear slung over my shoulder and the walk was a long one. As I approached the spires of the Downs my excitement grew. Being surrounded by eager party people already openly drunk at 10am adds to the excitement. Hundreds of National Guardsmen controlled traffic flow, stopped each cab and shuttle bus performing an under-carriage search with little shaving mirrors on telescoping sticks. My camera bag was thoroughly searched at the entrance by military personnel. I took some time to explain the other bag I was carrying, my blue jean man-purse with my Ozzy crap in it. I showed the nice army man my Ozzy card, and said that the Downs client requested I show up with it. With studied indifference he rifled through looking for explosives, I guess, but the most dangerous "weapon" I had was a large pointy crucifix on a chain. He waved me through.

Once inside I made my way upstairs to the executive offices where I was given my highly treasured (number 000033) "All Area Access" laminated pass to wear around my neck, giving me more access to more areas of the Downs than 99.9% of the 148,530 other people there that day. The tension level was high at Command Central. Our company had produced an online betting game for Derby weekend and the website was being hammered with 177,000+ simultaneous users choosing their horses for the Five Million Dollar Payday Game.

158

The deal was, if you could correctly guess the finishing order of each of the seventeen horses in the 129th Kentucky Derby—from the winner to last place—you would win five million dollars.

Needless to say there was a lot of security built into the online game and there were teams of auditors, etc., to assure that it wasn't going to be hacked and that any win would be a real one. Of course, the odds against putting that many horses in the right order were safely astronomical, but I found it interesting that Lloyds of London insured the possibility of a five million dollar payout for only twenty-grand. (Nobody won the prize.) About an hour before the race when the online traffic was spiking, the game was hanging up for some reason. The programmer who wrote the code was vacationing in Copenhagen when the distress call went out. We had a programmer on the other side of the world, dialing in with his laptop through lousy European phone lines, dropping out every few minutes or so, trying to make changes in the game's code "on the fly," in real time.

There was a lot riding on the success of the game for the Downs and for my company and things got heated. I welcomed my assignment of roaming Millionaire's Row because it gave me an excuse to get as far away from this tense technical noise as I could.

I wasn't getting as many interviews as I would have liked. I encountered incredible police resistance trying to tape Janet Jackson, even from a distance, so I gave up before I got banned from the space. Tim Allen pretty much told me to get lost. I missed the opportunity to grab a quote from Steven Spielberg, as he brushed past me so fast. I managed to interview Sigourney Weaver, Travis Tritt, 'N Sync's Chris Kirkpatrick and Joey Fatone, Larry King, Taylor Dayne, Joe Millionaire, Toby Keith, Mathew St. Patrick, Michael Bloomberg (who consulted with his lawyer as to whether he could answer the question on camera "Who are you betting in the Derby race?"), U.S. Secretary of Labor Elaine Chao, Dallas Cowboys quarterback Troy Aikman, George Strait, Pamela Anderson with her date Kid Rock (whose betting "strategy" consisted of putting $100 on each and every horse) and the large yet absolutely radiant Anna Nicole Smith.

By my third trip back to the offices to upload more celebrity videos the guys had figured out the problems with the online game, the programmer on the other side of the planet had gone back to sleep and my boss had started to breathe normally again. The day was progressing nicely.

I'm not a gambling man, but it's hard not to put a few bucks on the Derby. I generally bet on the jockey instead of the horse, since I don't know how to bet in the first place. Pat Day seemed to me to be the modern-day Willie Shoemaker and I decided to put a few bucks on his horse for the Run for the Roses. A lot of good it did. I watched the big race from the Churchill offices. By that time of day we had stopped putting up new video clips on the site and were preparing for the posting of the fresh finish line action shot of the winner. One of the sports writers in the office erupted in hoots and hollers as Funny Cide crossed the finish line. He had the horse bet six ways from breakfast and was quite proud of himself. Funny Cide was a long shot, ($27.60 win, $12.40 place and $8.20 show...and that's on a $2.00 bet before all the boxing and trifecta action I don't understand gets going—and the writer had it going).

At this point my workday was over. I had my Ozzy crap in my man-purse but really wasn't going to bring it up. Jeremy, the Kentucky Derby webmaster, hadn't forgotten. He turned to me and said, "Now would be a good time to get Ozzy out." In the warm afterglow of a long and tense day gone well, the Donning of the Ozzy Gear filled me with positive anticipation. The only thing I worried about was creating a scene and getting my company in trouble for causing a disruption. There were still jitters about terrorism and the place was crawling with National Guardsmen and police, so there was a definite line that shouldn't be crossed. Problem was no one had any idea where that line was.

It doesn't take very long at all to let my hair down, change into my blue glasses, pull on the black tee shirt and exercise pants and hang some chains around my neck. I didn't bother writing O Z Z Y on my knuckles because I didn't think I'd get close enough to anyone for it to matter. They led me out on the balcony of Churchill Downs that overlooks the front of the racetrack. There were a couple of additional races on the card that day, but after The Derby a lot of tourists head home, so the crowd was streaming out of the turnstiles beneath the third floor veranda where I emerged.

I threw my hands up and yelled as loud as I could, "Rock and rollll....Kentucky Derby!!...I love you all!" Whether or not I could be heard below mattered little as soon as someone turned around and saw me up there. I was sufficiently far enough away that the illusion was a good one, and word spread like wildfire through the crowd that stopped dead in its tracks, turned en masse, and started yelling back. I waived my arms and ran back and forth screaming. The crowd roared. I got so into it that I put my man-purse, with my car keys, wallet and real glasses, on the ledge precariously balanced and ready to go over into a crowd of strangers three stories below. Thankfully I came to my senses long enough to pull it down, scolding myself in the process not to lose it completely, my wallet or my mind.

After a couple of minutes I didn't want to let the illusion rot, so I shuffled inside the offices. Downs employees were standing around laughing at the scene I'd caused. It seemed to be thumbs up all around. Drunk dignitaries were slapping me on the back as I made my way through the office hallways. "Let's do the outfield," Jeremy suggested. "I'm up for it," I responded, and we ducked down a long stairwell leading to the grandstands. Jeremy, as the fake bodyguard was to lead, with dark glasses and his cell phone earphone in place to complete the illusion. I had wanted several large men around me not just for looks—but to fend off the thousands of drunks we were about to encounter. Only one other guy besides Jeremy, one of the website photographers, was crazy enough to come with us. He wanted to take video, which suited me fine. The only other protection I would have would be a young woman who had been helping out with website duties. She volunteered to watch my back as we moved through the crowd. My security was thin.

My instructions were clear and concise, "Don't let anyone get too close to me, no touching, stay between me and the general public, keep moving at all costs, and if things get ugly run." As we worked our way through the crowd toward the entrance to the outfield, not making any effort to call attention to ourselves, the occasional "Hey, that's Ozzy Osbourne dude, right there!" could be heard as we kept lurching forward.

The Churchill Downs infield is a legendary lawn inside the race-track's circle where thousands of drunks celebrate Derby Day, most never seeing a single horse. Considered the "cheap seats" (although this year it was $28.00 per person for the privilege). Many arrive early on Derby Day, throw down a blanket and make it an all-day picnic. By late afternoon the scene resembles a small-scale Woodstock (after the rain storm). Drunks wander aimlessly, a bandstand entertains the young folks, scores of others perch on bleachers, trying to see a little bit of the track, but mostly it's a party on the scale of a large rock festival with horses occasionally running around the outside.

Into this roiling mass of humanity wades The Fake Ozzy. There is a long tunnel that leads from the grandstands, under the racetrack, then up and out onto the infield. While our little group of four made its way through this tunnel, word spread quickly, with drunks running past us to announce, "It's Ozzy! It's fucking Ozzy Osbourne! Woo-hoo!!!" Young men flew past us screaming, "I love you Ozzy, I love your show! You're the shit," etc., that tipped off folks in front who started to amass at the mouth of the tunnel to greet us. This wasn't looking good to me. Too many people, too close, people are touching me, getting too good of a look. Yet the screaming continued to build in volume, and everyone still had smiles on their faces so out into the infield we headed. I kept looking for a radio station promotional booth or something we could duck into to get behind any kind of security barrier. A little bit of distance is important for maintaining the illusion. But I couldn't see any, and when I heard someone yell, "*That's* not Ozzy," I felt it was time to return to Command Central and fast. "Move move move!" I yelled to my "security staff." We wheeled around back toward the tunnel entrance and worked our way back through the crowd that by now was screaming, "Ozzy! Ozzy! Ozzy!" in unison. On the way back upstairs to the offices we paused to pose for photos with a few National Guardsmen who didn't look too amused by the disturbance we were causing.

Safely behind the doors of the offices it was laughter all around. The cool thing about having "bodyguards" along is that there is no way to explain the excitement and adrenaline that happens in this kind of situation, so having a couple of objective viewpoints experience the same thing helps me reality-check the level of craziness. Jeremy was laughing pretty hard as I stepped back out on the veranda for one more wave at the crowd. "Watch me light 'em up," I said, a phrase I borrowed from a George H. Bush interview I read about how he used to be able to simply point to a section of a crowd and cause it to erupt in cheers. It actually works. And it's more fun than you can imagine.

We hadn't been on our infield trip more than fifteen minutes but the word had obviously spread among the people in front of the

Downs that Ozzy was upstairs. When I came out the second time, the crowd was twice as big as before. A roar went up with my arms as I started shouting "I love you all!" I have to admit that I went a bit out of control up there (I blame it on the mint juleps). I felt like Mussolini. The crowd couldn't hear the individual words I was saying—I could have been yelling "Cream cheese!" and they'd still be waving back and taking photos.

This continued for a few minutes and things were getting more frantic. The folks up on the balcony knew it was a goof, so they were all enjoying the joke. The folks beneath thought they were seeing their one last celebrity at The Downs for the day and enjoying it from that angle. I was living my dream of being applauded for simply being, so I was enjoying the hell out of it. Then I took it one step too far. "Moon em!" someone yelled. I don't know who, but it seemed like a good idea at the time. I turned my back to the railing, slid my pants down just a bit and the crowd went ape shit. "That's as good a place to leave it as any," I thought and went back inside to much laughter. Then two National Guardsmen walked into the office. "That's all for Ozzy," one said with a stern expression. I was already getting out of my gear and I said, "Right, we're through." He mentioned that it was all fine up until the moon came out and the reaction of the crowd at that point was such that the Guard felt it was time to "bring a degree of control to the situation." A national security risk: my ass.

The walk back to the car was easier than the morning's walk to the Downs. I'd done my job for the website, did the Ozzy routine to the delight of our clients, and got out alive. I didn't win any money on the race, but I'd had one heck of a good time. When I got home I showed my parents the video of me running around the infield and up on the balcony. "It was only a half-moon Dad, really." My 89 year-old father could only shake his head in disbelief. He feigned disapproval but couldn't hide his smile.

11

Mamma I'm Coming Home

"I never set out to be a businessman.
I just wanted to have fun, fuck chicks and do drugs."
- Ozzy Osbourne

One of the questions about my look-alike experience that comes up a lot is "How much money did you make?" Not much, maybe broke even, but that's not why I did it. It started off pretty lopsided:

$250.00 – Povy's photo session

$69.82 – scans and prints of photos

$188.00 – reference DVDs and CDs

$93.00 – OzzFest ticket (research)

$75.00 – haircut and dye job (including huge tip)

$116.00 – initial trip to The Ritz for jewelry and makeup

$330.00 – first look-alike convention

$280.00 –Vegas flight

$13.58 – two Stunt Doves

$150 – reverend's coat, hair dye, various
Ozzy tee shirts

$215.28 – Wilson's Leather, coat and pants

$233.00 – flight to New York to do MTV's
Wannabes

$332.00 – The Chelsea Savoy

$12.99 – the right eye makeup

$68.64 – Ellen's Stardust Diner with
Robert De Niro

$94.39 – red wigs, hair clips, more chains
and crosses from The Ritz

. . . add the two additional round trips to Vegas and the two convention fees, plus The Reel Awards and the Hollywood expenses—obviously I wasn't in it for the money. Not that I didn't have opportunities from time to time. I could get an offer of a grand plus expenses for an out of town job but they were usually in the middle of the week, and the number of vacation days (minimum two) that I would have had to use offset the fee for the most part. Largely I felt that unless it was for a national television show I really wasn't interested.

Yet even with the offers I'd turned down over the course of 2002 when Ozzy was at his hottest, it didn't look like it was a steady enough income stream to bother with the paperwork and extra CPA fees to make a legitimate business out of it. Besides, the head trip it was giving me just doing the odd stunt or getting together with other bizarre people was, after all was said and done, cheaper than therapy and a hell of a lot more fun.

Professionally, I acquiesced to a New York socialite wedding (I wanted to do a paying gig to see what it was like), a couple of car commercials in Kansas City (I'd end up with some fun video footage), an employee appreciation dinner in Denver (it was close by and easy)—a grand total of twenty-five hundred dollars in performance fees over a year and a half. I probably turned down five to eight grand in work during that time but money wasn't my focus. I felt as if I was almost seeking some kind of peace, some kind of revelation, an understanding of the forces that could drive a grown man to wear eyeliner and make faces for photographs with strangers.

The profound effect it had on my view of fame, celebrity, performing for a living and show business in general was the real education I received for my expensive "tuition." By the time I finally retired my Stunt Dove and hung up my rubber bat at the end of 2003, amazing things had happened to me that not even a kid watching Ed Sullivan could imagine. It was an overdose of the kind of attention I spent a lifetime dreaming about. It was more fun than I have ever had in my life, but at times I came dangerously close to losing my own identity in the craziness of the moment.

Along the way I learned a lot about the celebrity look-alike business and those who participate in it. I got a rare glimpse at how "fame" looked from the other side—from the perspective of the famous. Fame is something the outside world lends to an individual. It takes the cooperation of the public to create the phenomenon. I was lifted to a position afforded famous people simply by virtue of my appearance, in spite of my earnest attempts in Los Angeles through the years to earn it on my own.

Is fake fame no less satisfying than the real deal? All the sweetness and none of the calories? What did it feel like when my limo was surrounded by young co-eds, thrusting pens, pencils and pads through the window for my "autograph?" I felt like a rock star. In that moment it didn't matter to me that I wasn't who they thought I was. I was in my dream of dreams. While a dream isn't reality, it *is* while you're asleep. My take on it is, if someone thinks you're famous— then you are.

In a society that elevates individuals to celebrity status sometimes for simply being who they are (Paris Hilton, Anna Nicole Smith, et. al.) is there a "real" famous (*Ozzy earned it over a 30+ year career*) versus "fake" fame (*I was a poser*)? I think so. Do they feel different? At times I think not.

Does an audience require "the real thing" in order to be entertained? Obviously not—something else was going on. The people who actually thought I was the real Ozzy, I can understand. The people who knew I wasn't and *still* participated in the illusion by *behaving like* the real Ozzy was in their presence, interested me greatly. A friend of mine, Boulder iconoclast Robert Carl Cohen, summed it up for me by suggesting that this emotional response was simply a reptilian brain reaction to past pleasure. He explained it to me thusly:

Upon seeing Ozzy (or in my case, his likeness), Ozzy fans' brains release certain soothing chemicals that cause a feeling of happiness—happiness learned through multiple pleasurable experiences that went before, like attending one of his concerts or laughing at his television show. Therefore, even though they are gazing upon a known replica, there are still squirts of happy juice flowing into their gray matter, and they react in a primal way as if they are experiencing the real deal. At first I thought my friend was nuts, but I found myself in more and more situations where I witnessed first hand what he had described.

Another friend of mine, Carlos Espinosa, who holds a Psychology degree in Existential Phenomenology, reacted thusly when I told him of my adventures:

> Now, what you get to exercise is a fundamental existential principle—you are exercising your ontological freedom. This is power. This is something FEW of us really get to do. To have the ability to set aside, or to bracket, ones throwness and to adopt a new schema, or attunement to the world—willingly and consciously—is rare. You have that ability to perceive, behave and react to objects, situations and others in a manner which is different than your true throwness (throwness is, basically, how you behave, see, define and act in the world—it is where you are going, where you have been and how you have been involved—for the most part you have no control over your throwness but you do have the ability to accept it, struggle against it, reject it or completely deny it... no matter whether you 'like' it or not you can't change that fact, as an example, that you were born to a carnival freak under a railroad car in Canada). However, unlike that carnival freak, you CHOOSE to do this!

> So think about this. Your ability to place yourself "into the shoes" of another individual, to be seen, treated

and accepted as someone other than yourself is truly rare, and, well, just awesome! Think of all those that you know who sit at their desk day after day and stare out the window continually wishing to be somewhere else, dreaming of being able to escape—to travel and get the royal treatment, to be treated as a celebrity, as royalty—if only for a day. Think of those, as grandma, who cannot move out of their 'altered' mode, who cannot control their shift in behavior or attunement, who have no control over when and how they behave, who are not aware of any sort of change in reality they are experiencing... For you to be able to shift into this mode, to bracket your throwness and move into a new attunement, to make a conscious shift in your perceptual reality... man, that is unreal. UNREAL!!

To me, and many others, this ability is the 'ultimate power' in that it is control not over others, but over your self.

Heady stuff. I didn't realize I was "bracketing my throwness," I was just trying to have fun, or so I rationalized.

In the end I felt a bit upstaged by what I was imitating. You can only graciously receive applause for someone else a certain amount of time before it begins to wear on your soul. Friends would invite me to parties with the caveat: "Oh, you'll be coming dressed as Ozzy yeah?" They weren't inviting me—they were inviting my clown act. This had to end. It was time to hang up my rubber Stunt Bat.
I still had enough of a ponytail to donate to Locks of Love to benefit little kids with cancer. I left the round glasses on the bottom of the Boulder Reservoir and bought some rectangular frames from a Belgian madman named Theo. I didn't look like Ozzy anymore. My Ozzy look-alike website changed to reflect my retirement from the celebrity look-alike business to a focus on this book that you hold. And I bid fond farewell to the best excuse I ever had for mindless overindulgence.

What, if anything did I learn from my Ozzy experiences, other than people are easily fooled when they want to be? I learned that fame can be largely false, because it can be based as much on an illusion as on talent or accomplishments. I learned that people love to be entertained so much that they will suspend their disbelief to an astonishing degree. I learned that if five people in a crowd of a thousand believe in something, they can cause the others to "see" it as real too. I even began to better understand how religion works.

At some point in the Ozzy look-alike madness it became clear to me that, as sad as it might sound, what I had experienced during that year was "it" for me. That it was as close as I was going to get to being a rich and famous rock star—as close as I was going to get to achieving my life long dream. This thought was potentially devastating but actually amused me upon greater reflection. Fate had handed me, at the very last possible moment I might add, in my 50s, a first class ticket on a roller coaster ride showing me from the inside what it could have been like.

My dilemma, my potential nightmare in fact, came down to how I was going to internalize the experience. Should I allow myself to feel like I had reached my goal of achieving fame? Was the attention I received as a fake celebrity worthy of this? Was I insane not to let it be? And if I did allow myself to feel that I had achieved one of my largest Life Goals—a goal I went to bed with every night and woke up with every day, what then? Would that mean that I could, or more frighteningly, *would* have to come up with another, different, more realistically achievable goal to focus on for the remainder of my life?

In the end I realized that my 30-year longing, my prayer to the universe for fame was in fact answered, but not in the way I envisioned. I almost missed the message. It dawned on me that it is entirely possible to get what you have wanted your entire life and not recognize it. People may have their prayers answered, realize their own dream and not even know it—because it comes in a different package than they expected.

Dear DON,

Thank you for your generous hair donation! Your selfless act of kindness will benefit a Locks of Love recipient and change their life for the better. Most of our recipients suffer from an autoimmune disease called alopecia areata, which has no known cause or cure. Other recipients are cancer survivors, victims of trauma such as burns and rare dermatological conditions that result in permanent hair loss. Your donation of hair will help return smiles to the many varied faces of our children. On behalf of those children, their families and the Board of Directors,

THANK YOU - YOU MADE A DIFFERENCE!!

Madonna Coffman
President

About the Author

Don Wrege is a Boulder, Colorado-based multimedia producer with a record of professional success in media design and production management spanning three decades. Ranging from the beginnings of multimedia to the emergence of the Internet and interactive television, his clients have included: Pepsi, Whole Foods, Lands' End, FranklinCovey, Columbia Pictures, Warner Bros. Records, Capitol Records, Mattel, Jackson Browne and ABC Television. An ASCAP writer/publisher, in his spare time Wrege composes and records irritating parody songs for Denver's *Peter Boyles Show* and other Clear Channel radio personalities.

www.donwrege.com

For *My Year as Ozzy* look-alike video and audio files, more pictures and information please visit:

www.myyearasozzy.com